Advanced Maths Essentials
Decision 1 for AQA

Welcome to Advanced Maths Essentials: Decision 1 for AQA. This book will help you to improve your examination performance by focusing on all the essential maths skills you will need in your AQA Descision 1 examination. It has been divided by chapter into the main topics that need to be studied. Each chapter has then been divided by sub-headings, and the description below each sub-heading gives the AQA specification for that aspect of the topic.

The book contains scores of worked examples, each with clearly set-out steps to help solve the problem. You can then apply the steps to solve the Skills Check questions in the book and past exam questions at the end of each chapter. At the back of this book there is a sample exam-style paper to help you test yourself before the big day.

Pearson Education Limited
Edinburgh Gate
Harlow
Essex
CM20 2JE
England
www.longman.co.uk

First published 2005
ISBN   140581845X

Design by Ken Vail Graphic Design

Cover design by Raven Design

Typeset by Tech-Set, Gateshead

Printed in the U.K. by Scotprint, Haddington

The publisher's policy is to use paper manufactured from sustainable forests.

We are grateful for permission from the Assessment and Qualifications Alliance to reproduce past exam questions. All such questions have a reference in the margin. The Assessment and Qualifications Alliance can accept no responsibility whatsoever for accuracy of any solutions or answers to these questions.

Every effort has been made to ensure that the structure and level of sample question papers matches the current specification requirements and that solutions are accurate. However, the publisher can accept no responsibility whatsoever for accuracy of any solutions or answers to these questions. Any such solutions or answers may not necessarily constitute all possible solutions.

1 Simple ideas of algorithms

Correctness, finiteness and generality; stopping conditions.

An **algorithm** is an unambiguous set of instructions that may be given as a list, a flow chart, a program or in words. **Correctness** just means that the algorithm does what it is supposed to do in all cases.

Each algorithm requires an **input** (although sometimes this is just a 'start' command) and will produce an **output** (although sometimes this is just a 'finished' statement). Each input produces an output and if the same input is used again it will produce the same output – the output does not depend on anything other than the input.

Each algorithm must be **finite** (it must finish and not just keep looping round and round on itself) and there must be a **stopping condition** (although sometimes this is implied from having reached the end of the algorithm).

Tracing an algorithm

Tracing an algorithm means working through it by hand and recording the changes to the values of the variables.

Example 1.1   Consider the following algorithm:

LINE 10:   Input two positive integers A and B with $A > B$
LINE 20:   Give Q the value 0 and R the value of A
LINE 30:   Reduce R by B and increase Q by 1
LINE 40:   If $R < B$ go to LINE 50, otherwise go to LINE 30
LINE 50:   Output the values Q and R

This algorithm finds the quotient Q and remainder R when A is divided by B. This can be written $A = Q \times B + R$.

Trace through the algorithm using the values $A = 20$, $B = 7$.

Step 1: State the starting conditions.

Step 2: Write the results of each instruction. Show changes to the values of A, B, Q, R.

LINE	A	B	Q	R	Comments
10	20	7			Input given values
20			0	20	Initial values of Q and R
30			1	13	Update Q and R
40					$R \geqslant B$ so repeat LINE 30
30			2	6	
40					$R < B$ so we go to LINE 50
50			2	6	Output values

Tip:
You can display each line in a table for clarity.

Note:
It is not always necessary to list the line numbers and we do not always need to give comments.

Completing an algorithm

Completing an algorithm means finishing off an algorithm that has already been started for you. You will not be expected to write a complete algorithm without it having been started for you.

Example 1.2   The algorithm in Example 1.1 finds the quotient Q and remainder R when A is divided by B, i.e. $A = Q \times B + R$. If $R = 0$ then B is the highest common factor of A and B.

If $R \neq 0$ we can replace A by the value of B and B by the value of R and run the algorithm again. Eventually $R = 0$ and the algorithm stops.

Write down suitable instructions for LINE 60 and LINE 70 to complete the algorithm so that it outputs the highest common factor of A and B.

Step 1: Check if $R = 0$. If $R = 0$, output the value of B and stop.

Step 2: If $R \neq 0$ update the values of A and B and run the new values through the algorithm.

LINE 60:   If $R = 0$ then output B and STOP; otherwise go to LINE 70

LINE 70:   Replace A with the value of B and then replace B with the value of R, then go back to LINE 20

Note:
You must include 'and STOP' to prevent the algorithm from continuing after it should have finished.

Note:
You need to update A before you update B.

Amending an algorithm

Amending an algorithm means changing lines that have already been given, either to correct the given algorithm or to change what it does.

Example 1.3   When the algorithm in Example 1.1 is extended in Example 1.2 to find the highest common factor of A and B it is no longer necessary to keep a record of the values of Q. This is done by rewriting some of the lines of the original algorithm and removing any now redundant lines. Amend the algorithm by rewriting the lines that have changed and state which lines can be removed.

Step 1: Remove the references to Q in lines 20, 30 and 50.

Rewrite
LINE 20:   Give R the value A
LINE 30:   Reduce R by B
LINE 40:   If $R < B$ go to LINE 60, otherwise go to LINE 30
And remove LINE 50.

SKILLS CHECK   1A: Understanding algorithms

1   Trace the following algorithm.

LINE 10:   Let $A = 10$
LINE 20:   Let $B = A \div 2$
LINE 30:   Let $C = B \times B$
LINE 40:   If $C - A$ is between -0.1 and $+0.1$, jump to LINE 70, otherwise continue to LINE 50
LINE 50:   Replace B by $(B + (A \div B)) \div 2$
LINE 60:   Go back to LINE 30
LINE 70:   Display B
LINE 80:   Stop

2   It has been claimed that the algorithm below computes the prime factors of an input number.

LINE 10:   Input N [N must be a positive integer > 1]
LINE 20:   Let $P = 2$
LINE 30:   Let $D = \text{INT}(N \div P)$
LINE 40:   If $N = 1$ STOP

Note:
'INT' computes the integer part of a number, for example $\text{INT}(2.6) = 2$.

LINE 50:	If $N = P \times D$ display P, otherwise go to LINE 80
LINE 60:	Let $N = D$
LINE 70:	Go to LINE 30
LINE 80:	Let $P = 3$
LINE 90:	Let $D = \text{INT}(N \div P)$
LINE 100:	If $N = 1$ STOP
LINE 110:	If $N = P \times D$ display P, otherwise go to LINE 140
LINE 120:	Let $N = D$
LINE 130:	Go to LINE 90
LINE 140:	Increase P by 2
LINE 150:	Go to LINE 90

Trace through the algorithm using $N = 60$.

3 In the algorithm in question **2**, explain the purpose of

   a LINE 40   **b** LINE 50

   c LINE 20 to LINE 50   **d** LINE 60 and LINE 70.

4 Apply the following algorithm to the list of numbers below.

    28, 64, 37, 59, 21, 54, 47, 33

LINE 10:	Let $N = 8$
LINE 20:	Set $N = N \div 2$ and $C = 1$
LINE 30:	Extract from the list the numbers in positions $C, C + N, C + 2N, \ldots$
LINE 40:	Sort the numbers in the sublist, then insert the numbers in the sublist back into the original list in positions $C, C + N, C + 2N, \ldots$
LINE 50:	Increase C by 1
	If C is less than or equal to N go back to LINE 30, otherwise continue to LINE 60
LINE 60:	If $N = 1$ stop and print out the list, otherwise go back to LINE 20

Show your results in the form of a table.

5 Trace the following algorithm when $N = 17$.

LINE 10:	Input a positive integer N
LINE 20:	Print the value of N
LINE 30:	Let $C = 0$
LINE 40:	If N is even, replace N by $N \div 2$
	Otherwise replace N by $3N + 1$
LINE 50:	Replace C by $C + 1$
LINE 60:	Print the value of N
LINE 70:	If N does not equal 1, go back to LINE 40
LINE 80:	If N equals 1, output the value of C and stop

6 Apply the following algorithm to the list 8, 12, 8, 13, 9.

LINE 10:	Let $N = 0$, $A = 0$ and $B = 0$
LINE 20:	Let $N = N + 1$
LINE 30:	Let X be the first item in the list
LINE 40:	Let $A = A + X$ and let $B = B + X^2$
LINE 50:	Delete the first item from the list
LINE 60:	If the list is not empty, go to LINE 20
LINE 70:	Let $S = B - (A^2 \div N)$
LINE 80:	Let $M = A \div N$
LINE 90:	Let $D = \sqrt{(S \div (N - 1))}$
LINE 100:	Display M, D

7 Find the output of the following algorithm when $A = 3$, $D = 2$ and $N = 5$.

LINE 10:	Let $C = 1$, $T = A$ and $S = A$
LINE 20:	Display the value of T
LINE 30:	If $C = N$ go to LINE 80
LINE 40:	Let $C = C + 1$
LINE 50:	Let $T = T + D$
LINE 60:	Let $S = S + T$
LINE 70:	Go to LINE 20
LINE 80:	Print "Sum equals"
LINE 90:	Display the value of S
LINE 100:	STOP

8 The following algorithm is intended to generate the Fibonacci sequence 1, 1, 2, 3, 5, 8, 13, 21, 34, 55, … in which the first two terms are 1 and the remaining terms are formed by summing the two previous terms.

LINE 10:	Let $A = 1$ and $B = 1$
LINE 20:	Print the value of A and the value of B
LINE 30:	Replace A by $A + B$
LINE 40:	Print the value of A
LINE 50:	Go back to LINE 30

a Trace this algorithm to print out the first ten terms of the sequence.

b Show how to amend the algorithm so that it stops when it has printed ten terms.

c Show how the algorithm can be corrected so that it displays the Fibonacci sequence.

1.2 Types of algorithm

Bubble, shuttle, shell, quicksort algorithms.

There are many different algorithms that can be used to sort a list of items into order (for example, sort numbers into increasing, or ascending, order). Most sorting algorithms consist of making a number of passes through the list of items to be sorted.

You can compare different sorting algorithms by counting the number of times items are compared and swapped.

Bubble sort

In bubble sort, the first pass involves comparing the first and second items and swapping if necessary, then comparing whatever is now the second item with the third item and swapping if necessary, then comparing whatever is now third with the fourth item and swapping if necessary, and so on until the last item has been considered.

After the first pass, the item that is now in the last place will be correctly positioned. Some other items in the list may also be correctly positioned but at this stage only the position of the last item can be guaranteed.

In the second pass, do the same thing, but stop when the last item but one has been considered (as the final item is guaranteed, we stop at the last item that we cannot guarantee).

Continue like this, using ever shorter lists of items to compare until either a list of only one item is reached (because all the other items are guaranteed to be correctly positioned), or a pass is made in which no items are swapped (in which case the entire list is guaranteed to be sorted).

Example 1.4   Use bubble sort to sort the list 6, 4, 8, 2, 3, 7, 4 into ascending order.

6 4 8 2 3 7 4

Step 1: Make a first pass through the list.

First pass:

4 6 8 2 3 7 4	Is 6 ≤ 4? No, swap 6 and 4
4 6 8 2 3 7 4	Is 6 ≤ 8? Yes, no change
4 6 2 8 3 7 4	Is 8 ≤ 2? No, swap 8 and 2
4 6 2 3 8 7 4	Is 8 ≤ 3? No, swap 8 and 3
4 6 2 3 7 8 4	Is 8 ≤ 7? No, swap 8 and 7
4 6 2 3 7 4 8	Is 8 ≤ 4? No, swap 8 and 4

Note:
Here underlining indicates items that have been compared, and bold shows the items that are guaranteed to be in the correct places.

Step 2: Fix the last item.

After first pass: 4 6 2 3 7 4 **8**

Step 3: Make a second pass through the reduced list.

Second pass:

4 6 2 3 7 4 **8**	Is 4 ≤ 6? Yes, no change
4 2 6 3 7 4 **8**	Is 6 ≤ 2? No, swap 6 and 2
4 2 3 6 7 4 **8**	Is 6 ≤ 3? No, swap 6 and 3
4 2 3 6 7 4 **8**	Is 6 ≤ 7? Yes, no change
4 2 3 6 4 7 **8**	Is 7 ≤ 4? No, swap 7 and 4

After second pass: 4 2 3 6 4 **7 8**

Step 4: Continue to pass through the list until either no swaps are made in a pass or the unsorted list is just a single item.

Third pass:

2 4 3 6 4 **7 8**	Is 4 ≤ 2? No, swap 4 and 2
2 3 4 6 4 **7 8**	Is 4 ≤ 3? No, swap 4 and 3
2 3 4 6 4 **7 8**	Is 4 ≤ 6? Yes, no change
2 3 4 4 6 **7 8**	Is 6 ≤ 4? No, swap 6 and 4

After third pass: 2 3 4 4 **6 7 8**

Note:
After three passes the list is sorted but the method hasn't revealed this yet. No swaps were made in the fourth pass – this is how the bubble sort shows that the list is now sorted.

Fourth pass:

2 3 4 4 **6 7 8**	Is 2 ≤ 3? Yes, no change
2 3 4 4 **6 7 8**	Is 3 ≤ 4? Yes, no change
2 3 4 4 **6 7 8**	Is 4 ≤ 4? Yes, no change

After fourth pass: **2 3 4 4 6 7 8**

Total: 18 comparisons and 11 swaps.

Shuttle sort

In the first pass through a **shuttle sort** compare the first and second items in the list and swap if necessary. In the second pass compare the second and third items and swap if necessary. If a swap is made shuttle back to compare the first and second items and swap if necessary. In the third pass compare the third and fourth items and swap if necessary. If a swap is made shuttle back to compare the second and third items and swap if necessary, and if a swap is made here shuttle back to compare the first and second items and swap if necessary. Continue in this way until the entire list has been passed through.

The effect of the kth pass is to pick up the item in position $k + 1$ in the original list and insert it in the correct position in the already sorted list of the first k items.

The shuttle sort cannot be stopped early, because the entire list must be passed through to find out whether the items at the end are big or small.

Example 1.5 Use shuttle sort to sort the list 6, 4, 8, 2, 3, 7, 4 into ascending order.

6 4 8 2 3 7 4

Step 1: Compare the first and second items.

Step 2: Move along the list one position.

Step 3: When a swap happens shuttle back until the item reaches its appropriate position and no swap is needed.

First pass: **4** 6 8 2 3 7 4   Is $6 \leqslant 4$? No, swap 6 and 4

Second pass: 4 **6 8** 2 3 7 4   Is $6 \leqslant 8$? Yes, no change

Third pass: 4 6 **2 8** 3 7 4   Is $8 \leqslant 2$? No, swap 8 and 2
            4 **2 6** 8 3 7 4   Is $6 \leqslant 2$? No, swap 6 and 2
            2 4 6 8 3 7 4   Is $4 \leqslant 2$? No, swap 4 and 2

Fourth pass: 2 4 6 **3 8** 7 4   Is $8 \leqslant 3$? No, swap 8 and 3
            2 4 **3 6** 8 7 4   Is $6 \leqslant 3$? No, swap 6 and 3
            2 **3 4** 6 8 7 4   Is $4 \leqslant 3$? No, swap 4 and 3
            2 3 4 6 8 7 4   Is $2 \leqslant 3$? Yes, no change.

Fifth pass: 2 3 4 6 **7 8** 4   Is $8 \leqslant 7$? No, swap 8 and 7
            2 3 4 **6 7** 8 4   Is $6 \leqslant 7$? Yes, no change

Sixth pass: 2 3 4 6 7 **4 8**   Is $8 \leqslant 4$? No, swap 8 and 4
            2 3 4 6 **4 7** 8   Is $7 \leqslant 4$? No, swap 7 and 4
            2 3 4 **4 6** 7 8   Is $6 \leqslant 4$? No, swap 6 and 4
            2 3 **4 4** 6 7 8   Is $4 \leqslant 4$? Yes, no change

Note:
Here bold shows items that are being shuttled.

Note:
No swap is made in the second pass so go straight on to the next pass.

Note:
In the third pass the item **2** shuttles into its correct place in the sorted sublist 4, 6, 8.

Note:
In the fifth pass item 7 has reached its correct place because it does not swap with 6.

Total: 15 comparisons and 11 swaps.

In this case, shuttle sort has fewer comparisons but the same number of swaps as bubble sort.

Shell sort

In the first pass through shell sort for a list of *n* items, compute $N = n \div 2$ and ignore any remainder. Extract the first item and every *N*th item starting from there. Sort this sublist using shuttle sort and insert the sorted sublist back into the spaces in the original list. Then extract the second item and every *N*th item from there and do the same thing. Continue in this way until every item in the original list has been considered.

In the second pass, do the same thing, but this time use $N = $ previous value $\div 2$, ignoring any remainder. Continue in this way to pass through the entire list with an *N* value equal to 1.

In shell sort, a long list is split into shorter sublists and then shuttle sort is applied to each sublist. The sublists are then merged back together. Shell sort is usually quicker than bubble sort or shuttle sort for very long lists.

Example 1.6 Use shell sort to sort the list 6, 4, 8, 2, 3, 7, 4 into ascending order.

Step 1: Compute $N = n \div 2$, ignoring any remainder.

$N = 7 \div 2 = 3$, ignoring the remainder.

Step 2: Extract first item and every Nth item after that.

Step 3: Drop sorted values into positions 1, $N + 1$, …

Step 4: Extract the second item and every Nth item after that.

Step 5: Drop sorted values into positions 2, $N + 2$, …

Step 6: Continue until all items have dropped down into place.

	6 4 8 2 3 7 4	Comp.	Swaps
First sublist:	6 2 4		
Sorted:	2 4 6	3	2
Second sublist:	4 3		
Sorted:	2 3 4 4 6	1	1
Third sublist:	8 7		
Sorted:	7 8	1	1
New list:	2 3 7 4 4 8 6		

Step 7: Compute a new value of N and work through the process again.

$N = 3 \div 2 = 1$, ignoring the remainder

Second pass	2 3 7 4 4 8 6	Comp.	Swaps
	2 3 4 4 6 7 8	10	4

Total: 15 comparisons, 8 swaps.

Shell sort generally requires fewer comparisons than shuttle sort or bubble sort. It works best when there are no remainders (when n is a power of 2).

Example 1.7 Use shell sort to sort the list 6, 4, 8, 2, 3, 7, 4, 1 into ascending order.

Step 1: Compute N. $N = 8 \div 2 = 4$

Step 2: Carry out first pass.

First pass:	6 4 8 2 3 7 4 1	C	S
	6 3	1	1
	4 7	1	0
	8 4	1	1
	2 1	1	1
New list:	3 4 4 1 6 7 8 2		

Step 3: Compute new value for N. $N = 4 \div 2 = 2$

Step 4: Carry out second pass.

Second pass:	3 4 4 1 6 7 8 2	C	S
	3 4 6 8	3	0
	4 1 7 2	5	3
New list:	3 1 4 2 6 4 8 7		

Step 5: Compute new value for N. $N = 2 \div 2 = 1$

Step 6: Carry out third pass.

Third pass:	3 1 4 2 6 4 8 7	C	S
Final list:	1 2 3 4 4 6 7 8	11	5

Total: 23 comparisons, 11 swaps.

Quicksort

In the first pass through quicksort, set the first item of the list to be the 'pivot', create two sublists, one of items that should come before (are less than) the pivot and the other of items that should come after (are greater than) the pivot.

In the second pass, repeat the process for each of the sublists. Continue in this way until each sublist consists of at most one item.

Note:
The pivot need not be the first item in the list; for a completely muddled up list it could just as well be, say, the middle item.

Example 1.8 Use quicksort to sort the list 6, 4, 8, 2, 3, 7, 4, 1 into ascending order.

Step 1: Locate the first item (the pivot).

Step 2: Sort the list into items that are less than and items that are greater than the pivot value.

Step 3: Fix the pivot and sort the sublists either side of it in the same way.

Step 4: Repeat until all sublists have length at most 1.

Note:
Here boxes indicate fixed items and underlining indicates the pivot.

	6	4	8	2	3	7	4	1
First pass:	4	2	3	4	1	[6]	8	7
Second pass:	2	3	1	[4]	4	[6]	7	[8]
Third pass:	1	[2]	3	[4]	[4]	[6]	[7]	[8]
Fourth pass	[1]	[2]	[3]	[4]	[4]	[6]	[7]	[8]

Example 1.9 Use quicksort to sort the list 6, 4, 8, 5, 3, 7, 4, 1 into ascending order.

Step 1: Locate pivot and sort items into lists either side of pivot.

Step 2: Sort the list into items that are less than and items that are greater than the pivot value.

Step 3: Continue until all sublists have length at most 1.

	6	4	8	5	3	7	4	1
First pass:	4	5	3	4	1	[6]	8	7
Second pass:	3	1	[4]	5	4	[6]	7	[8]
Third pass:	1	[3]	[4]	4	[5]	[6]	[7]	[8]
Fourth pass:	[1]	[3]	[4]	[4]	[5]	[6]	[7]	[8]

SKILLS CHECK 1B: Types of algorithm

1 Use bubble sort to rearrange the list of numbers 4, 5, 3, 1, 2 into ascending order. Show every stage of each pass that you make.

2 Use shuttle sort to rearrange the list of numbers 4, 7, 6, 4, 2, 5 into ascending order. You only need to show the result at the end of each pass.

3 Use the quicksort algorithm to rearrange the following list of numbers into ascending order: 6, 3, 5, 7, 4, 8, 1, 2, 9. Indicate the entries that you have used as pivots.

4 **a** Use shuttle sort to rearrange the list of numbers 31, 17, 25, 13, 21, 34 into descending order. Show the result at the end of each pass.

   b Count the number of swaps made in each pass and give the total number of swaps. What is the maximum number of swaps for a list of six numbers?

5 a Use shell sort to sort the list 8, 7, 6, 5, 4, 3, 2, 1 into ascending order.

b Count the number of comparisons and the number of swaps that were used when sorting the list into ascending order with shell sort, assume that shuttle sort is used to sort the sublists.

c Compare the number of comparisons used when sorting the list into ascending order with shell sort with the number used when sorting it with bubble sort.

6 Use quicksort to sot the list 4, 3, 7, 2, 7, 1, 8 into ascending order.

7 Use shell sort to sort the list 3, 5, 8, 3, 2, 4, 8, 3, 2 into ascending order.

8 Use shuttle sort to sort the list 3, 5, 4, 5, 2, 3, 6 into descending order. Show every swap that is made.

Examination practice   Simple ideas of algorithms

1 Use the Quicksort algorithm to rearrange the following list of flowers into alphabetical order. Rose (R), Iris (I), Wallflower (W), Dahlia (D), Pansy (P), Lobelia (L), Azalea (A). Indicate entries that you have used as pivots.   [AQA(A) June 2001]

2 a Trace the following algorithm.

Line 1	$A = 1$
Line 2	LABEL X
Line 3	$B = A*A*A$
Line 4	IF $B > 100$ THEN GOTO Y
Line 5	PRINT A, B
Line 6	$A = A + 1$
Line 7	GOTO X
Line 8	LABEL Y
Line 9	STOP

b Explain how your trace table would change if lines 1 and 2 were interchanged.
    [AQA(A) June 2001]

3 A student is using the algorithm below to find the real roots of a quadratic equation.

LINE 10	INPUT A, B, C
LINE 20	$D = B*B - 4*A*C$
LINE 30	$X_1 = (-B + \sqrt{D})/(2*A)$
LINE 40	$X_2 = (-B + \sqrt{D})/(2*A)$
LINE 50	IF $X_1 = X_2$ THEN GOTO L
LINE 60	PRINT "DIFFERENT ROOTS", X_1, X_2
LINE 70	GOTO M
LINE 80	LABEL L
LINE 90	PRINT "EQUAL ROOTS", X_1
LINE 100	LABEL M
LINE 110	END

a Trace the algorithm
   i if $A = 1, B = -4, C = 4$ **ii** if $A = 2, B = 9, C = 9$.

b **i** Find a set of values of A, B and C for which the algorithm would fail.
   ii Write down additional lines to ensure that the algorithm would not fail for **any** values of A, B and C that may be input.   [AQA(A) Jan 2002]

4 Use a Shell sort algorithm to rearrange the following numbers into ascending order, showing the new arrangement after each pass.

     14,   27,   23,   36,   18,   25,   16,   66   [AQA(A) May 2002]

5 The algorithm below is used to generate a sequence of numbers.

LINE 10	INPUT A POSITIVE INTEGER N
LINE 20	PRINT N
LINE 30	IF N IS EVEN, LET $N = N \div 2$
LINE 40	PRINT N
LINE 50	IF N IS ODD, LET $N = N - 1$
LINE 60	PRINT N
LINE 70	IF $N > 0$ THEN GOTO LINE 30
LINE 80	END

a Trace the algorithm when $N = 6$.

b Trace the algorithm when $N = 4$.

6 Use the quicksort algorithm to rearrange the following list of numbers into ascending order:

87   64   92   35   16   41   23

Indicate the entries that you have used as pivots.

7 Use the shell sort algorithm to sort the following list of numbers into ascending order.

35   89   31   27   14   11   5   44

Write down the list that results at the end of each pass and count the number of swaps made in each pass.

8 Use shuttle sort to put the following list into increasing order.

89   24   71   56   28   67   43

Show the list that results after each pass and count the number of comparisons and swaps in each pass.

9 Use bubble sort to put the following list into increasing order.

9   4   1   6   8   7   3

Show the list that results after each pass and count the number of comparisons and swaps in each pass.

2 Graphs and networks

2.1 Elements of graphs

Vertices, edges.

In graph theory, the term 'graph' means a set of **vertices**, or nodes, connected by **edges**, or arcs.

 This graph has five vertices and four edges.

Graphs may have loops that connect a vertex to itself. They may also have multiple edges joining any two vertices.

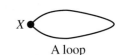
A loop

Multiple edges

A graph is made up of **subgraphs**. A subgraph is a graph in its own right and may consist of a vertex, two vertices and an edge, or many vertices and edges.

Some subgraphs of the graph on the right are given below.

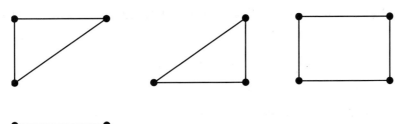

> **Note:**
> The actual positions of the vertices and the shapes of the edges do not matter.

Two graphs are equivalent, or **isomorphic**, if one can be transformed into the other without breaking any edges.

> **Note:**
> You will not be examined on isomorphic graphs but it is useful to know the terminology.

Example 2.1 Show that these two graphs are equivalent.

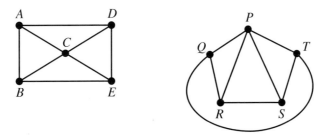

We need to topologically transform the graphs so that they look the same.

Step 1: Drop P down to sit between Q, R, S and T.

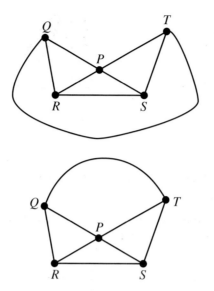

Step 2: Pull edge QT to the top to make the two graphs look the same.

> **Note:**
> We could relabel the second graph so that P becomes C, Q becomes A, R becomes B, S becomes E, and T becomes D.

The two graphs are the same. C and P are connected to each of the other four vertices, and every other vertex is connected to three other vertices.

2.2 Types of graph

Directed and undirected graphs; connectedness; bipartite graphs.

If a graph does not contain loops or multiple edges, it is called a **simple** graph.

Connected graphs

A **connected** graph is one where it is possible to reach any vertex from any other vertex, directly or indirectly.

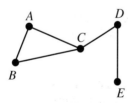   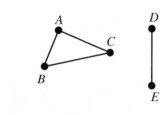

This graph is connected.   This graph is unconnected.

A graph that is not connected can be split into two or more disconnected subgraphs.

A graph that is both simple and connected is called a **simply connected** graph.

Directed and undirected graphs

In a **directed** graph, or digraph, some of the edges have a specific direction assigned (like a one-way street). A directed edge will be marked with an arrow to show its direction.

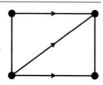

An **undirected** graph has no arrows. It can be represented as a directed graph as follows.

Planar graphs

A **planar graph** is one that can be drawn so that the edges do not cross over one another.

The graph on the left is planar because it can be transformed and redrawn as shown in the graph on the right.

Note:
You will not be examined on planar graphs but it is useful to know the terminology.

Bipartite graphs

The vertices of a **bipartite** graph can be split into two sets so that each edge joins a vertex from one set to a vertex from the other set; no edge joins two vertices which are in the same set. For example:

A **complete graph** of n vertices, K_n, is a simply connected graph where each vertex is connected to every other vertex by only one edge.

A **complete bipartite graph** $K_{m,n}$ is a simple bipartite graph with two sets of vertices, one of size m and the other of size n, in which every pair of vertices with one from each set are joined by an edge.

Example 2.2 Draw the graphs K_4 and K_5.

Step 1: Mark four vertices for K_4 and five for K_5, and connect every vertex to every other vertex.

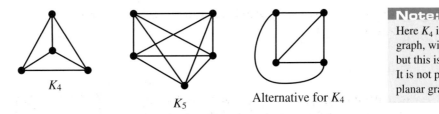

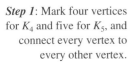

Note:
Here K_4 is shown as a planar graph, with no edges crossing, but this is not necessary.
It is not possible to draw K_5 as a planar graph.

13

Example 2.3 Draw the graph of $K_{3,4}$.

Step 1: Mark three vertices in a vertical line and four vertices in another vertical line and connect every vertex in one set to every vertex in the other set.

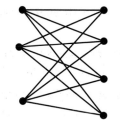

SKILLS CHECK **2A: Graphs**

1 Draw a diagram to show a connected graph with four vertices and five edges.

2 For each of the following:
 i give the number of vertices
 ii give the number of edges
 iii say whether or not the graph is connected.

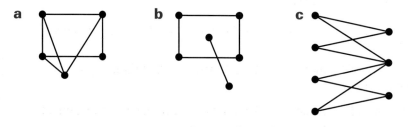

3 The graph K_4 has many subgraphs, several of which are isomorphic to one another. There are 10 non-isomorphic subgraphs (8 proper subgraphs, the subgraph with no edges and the subgraph that is the whole of K_4). Draw diagrams to illustrate the eight different proper subgraph types.

4 Consider the graphs drawn.

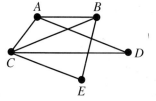 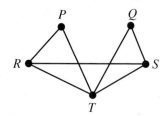

 a By relabelling the second graph, show that the two graphs are isomorphic.

 b By redrawing the first graph, show that the graphs are planar.

5 a Draw the graph $K_{3,3}$.

 b Delete any one edge from the graph $K_{3,3}$ and show that the resulting graph is planar.

6 a How many vertices and how many edges does the graph K_n have?

 b How many vertices and how many edges does the graph $K_{n,n}$ have?

 c How many vertices and how many edges does the graph $K_{m,n}$ have?

7 Draw an example of an undirected graph that has 4 vertices and 8 edges. Explain why there is no simple graph that fits this description.

8 Edges are removed from the graph K_5 to make a set of subgraphs that are not connected to one another.

    a What is the maximum number of edges that remain if there are two subgraphs, one connecting two vertices and one connecting three vertices?

    b What is the maximum number of edges that remain if there are two subgraphs, one connecting four vertices and the other consisting of a single vertex?

    c What is the maximum number of edges that remain if there are three subgraphs?

2.3 Adjacency matrices

Adjacency matrices.

Instead of a diagram, we may be given the information about which vertices are connected in an **adjacency matrix**.

In an adjacency matrix:

- an entry of '–' or '0' means there is no edge directly joining the two vertices

- an entry of '1' means that there is one edge that directly joins the two vertices

- an entry of '2' means that there are two different edges that directly join the two vertices, and so on.

Graphs with identical adjacency matrices are isomorphic.

> **Note:**
> Transforming graphs into matrices allows us to store the information in a computer.

Example 2.4 Represent the following graphs as adjacency matrices and hence show that they are isomorphic.

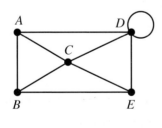

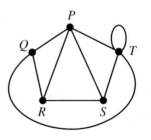

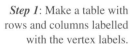
Step 1: Make a table with rows and columns labelled with the vertex labels.

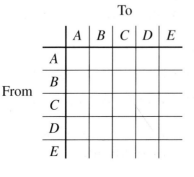

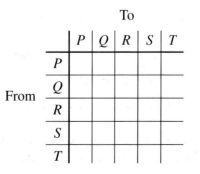

Step 2: For each vertex record the number of edges leading to each of the other vertices.

To

From	A	B	C	D	E
A	–	1	1	1	–
B	1	–	1	–	1
C	1	1	–	1	1
D	1	–	1	2	1
E	–	1	1	1	–

To

From	P	Q	R	S	T
P	–	1	1	1	1
Q	1	–	1	–	1
R	1	1	–	1	–
S	1	–	1	–	1
T	1	1	–	1	2

> **Note:**
> D to D is 2 and T to T is 2 because you can go either way around the loop.

Step 3: Reorder the rows and columns of the second matrix so that it looks the same as the first. This shows that the two graphs are the same.

To

From	A	B	C	D	E
A	–	1	1	1	–
B	1	–	1	–	1
C	1	1	–	1	1
D	1	–	1	2	1
E	–	1	1	1	–

To

From	Q	R	P	T	S
Q	–	1	1	1	–
R	1	–	1	–	1
P	1	1	–	1	1
T	1	–	1	2	1
S	–	1	1	1	–

> **Note:**
> If we sum across the rows of the tables we can see that A, B, E, Q, R, S and T have three edges coming from them and, C and P each have 4 edges and D and T have 5 edges.

SKILLS CHECK 2B: Adjacency matrices

1 Draw the graph represented by the adjacency matrix.

$$\begin{array}{c@{}c} & \begin{array}{cccc} A & B & C & D \end{array} \\ \begin{array}{c} A \\ B \\ C \\ D \end{array} & \left[\begin{array}{cccc} 0 & 1 & 0 & 2 \\ 1 & 0 & 2 & 1 \\ 0 & 2 & 0 & 1 \\ 2 & 1 & 1 & 0 \end{array} \right] \end{array}$$

2 A graph G is shown on the right.

Write down the adjacency matrix for this graph.

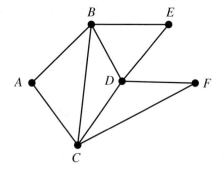

3 Draw the directed graph represented by this adjacency matrix.

$$\begin{array}{c@{}c} & \begin{array}{ccc} A & B & C \end{array} \\ \begin{array}{c} A \\ B \\ C \end{array} & \left[\begin{array}{ccc} 0 & 1 & 0 \\ 0 & 0 & 2 \\ 1 & 1 & 0 \end{array} \right] \end{array}$$

4 Write down the adjacency matrix for the graph shown.

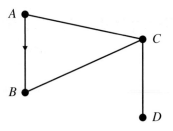

5 Write down the adjacency matrix for the graph K_4.

6 Draw the graph represented by this adjacency matrix.

$$
\begin{array}{c@{\quad}ccccc}
 & A & B & C & D & E \\
A & 0 & 2 & 1 & 2 & 1 \\
B & 2 & 0 & 1 & 0 & 1 \\
C & 1 & 1 & 2 & 1 & 1 \\
D & 2 & 0 & 1 & 0 & 1 \\
E & 1 & 1 & 1 & 1 & 0
\end{array}
$$

7 Write down the adjacency matrix for the graph $K_{2,2}$.

8 The adjacency matrices for three graphs are given below.

$$
\begin{array}{c@{\quad}cccc}
 & A & B & C & D \\
A & - & 1 & 2 & 1 \\
B & 1 & - & 1 & 2 \\
C & 2 & 1 & - & 1 \\
D & 1 & 2 & 1 & -
\end{array}
\qquad
\begin{array}{c@{\quad}cccc}
 & E & F & G & H \\
E & - & 1 & 1 & 1 \\
F & 1 & - & 1 & 2 \\
G & 1 & 1 & - & 2 \\
H & 1 & 2 & 2 & -
\end{array}
\qquad
\begin{array}{c@{\quad}cccc}
 & J & K & L & M \\
J & - & 1 & 2 & 1 \\
K & 1 & - & 1 & 1 \\
L & 2 & 1 & - & 2 \\
M & 1 & 1 & 2 & -
\end{array}
$$

  a By first considering the number of edges that connect to each vertex, show whether or not the graph represented by the first matrix is isomorphic to the graph represented by the second matrix.

  b Deduce whether either of the first two graphs is isomorphic to the third.

2.4 Degree of a vertex; trails, paths and cycles

Degree of a vertex, odd and even vertices; paths, cycles.

The **degree** of a vertex is the number of edges meeting at that vertex.
If the number of edges is even, the vertex is called an **even vertex**.
If the number of edges is odd, the vertex is called an **odd vertex**.

A **trail** is a sequence of edges such that the end vertex of one edge is the start vertex of the next.

A **path** is a trail with the additional restriction that no vertex is passed through more than once.

A **cycle** is a path to which an extra edge has been added to join the final vertex back to the initial vertex.

Note:
In a trail, a vertex can be passed through twice but an edge cannot be used twice.

Note:
A cycle is a closed path. In the Travelling Salesperson problem in Chapter 7, the word **tour** is used to describe a closed trail.

Example 2.5 For the graph shown on the right, give an example of:

  a a trail   **b** a path   **a** a cycle.

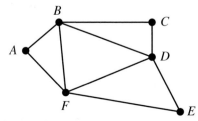

Step 1: Look for a sequence of edges where none of the edges are repeated.

a An example of a trail is $A - B - D - F - B - C$.

Note:
Vertex B is passed through twice but none of the edges are repeated.

Step 2: Look for a trail with no repeated vertices.

b An example of a path is $A - B - D - F$.

Step 3: Look for a path and add an edge to make the end point the same as the start.

c An example of a cycle is $A - B - D - F - A$.

Tip:
A trail or a path with just one edge is too simple to be useful.

SKILLS CHECK **2C: Degree of a vertex; trails, paths and cycles**

Questions **1**, **2** and **3** refer to the graph shown.

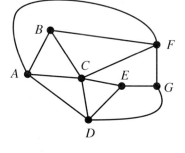

1 a Write down the degree of each vertex of the graph.

 b List the odd vertices.

 c Find the sum of the degrees of all the vertices and the number of edges in the graph.

2 For the graph above, write down an example of

 a a trail through four vertices, that is not also a path;

 b a path through four vertices;

 c a path through all the vertices.

3 For the graph above, explain why each of the following is **not** a cycle.

 a $A - B - C - D - E - F - G - A$

 b $A - B - C - D - E - G - F$

 c $A - B - C - D - E - C - A$

4 Draw an example of a connected graph with four vertices on which there are no cycles.

5 Draw a graph that has two vertices of degree 3 and two vertices of degree 1.

6 a Draw the graph represented by the following adjacency matrix.

$$
\begin{array}{c@{\quad}c}
 & \begin{array}{cccc} A & B & C & D \end{array} \\
\begin{array}{c} A \\ B \\ C \\ D \end{array} &
\left[\begin{array}{cccc}
0 & 2 & 0 & 1 \\
2 & 0 & 1 & 2 \\
0 & 1 & 0 & 1 \\
1 & 2 & 1 & 0
\end{array} \right]
\end{array}
$$

 b Write down an example of a path that passes through all four vertices on the graph.

 c Write down an example of a cycle that passes through all four vertices on the graph.

7 a Show that it is not possible to have an undirected graph with four vertices, one of degree 2 and three of degree 3.

b Draw a directed graph that has four vertices, one of degree 2 and three of degree 3.

8 Draw a graph that has four vertices on which there is a trail through all four vertices but there is no path through all four vertices.

2.5 Eulerian trails and Hamiltonian cycles

Eulerian trails and Hamiltonian cycles.

Eulerian trails

An **Eulerian** graph has a closed trail that contains every edge exactly once. A **semi-Eulerian** graph has a trail that is not closed but which contains every edge exactly once.

This graph is Eulerian.   This graph is not.

The easiest way to check whether a graph is Eulerian, semi-Eulerian or neither is to count the number of vertices of odd degree.
An Eulerian graph has no vertices of odd degree and a semi-Eulerian graph has exactly two vertices of odd degree.

Example 2.6 **a** Is the graph shown on the right Eulerian, semi-Eulerian or neither?

b What happens if an extra edge is added joining C to E?

Step 1: Count the degree of each vertex.

Step 2: Count the number of odd vertices.

Step 3: Amend the degrees of the vertices.

a A, C and E each have degree 2; B, D and F each have degree 4.

There are no odd vertices so the graph is Eulerian.

b With the extra edge, C and E become odd and the new graph is semi-Eulerian.

Any semi-Eulerian trail on this graph must have C and E as its initial and final vertices.

Hamiltonian cycles

A **Hamiltonian cycle** is a cycle that passes through every vertex exactly once and returns to the starting point.

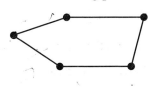

This is a Hamiltonian cycle.

Note:
A Hamiltonian cycle does not have to pass through every edge once.

Note:
Hamiltonian cycles are explored further in the Travelling Salesperson problem in Chapter 7.

1 A connected graph G has n vertices. State the minimum number of edges in a Hamiltonian cycle.

2 A connected graph G has six vertices. The degrees of the vertices are 2, 3, 4, 5, 6 and d.

    a The graph is semi-Eulerian. What can you say about the value of d?

    b The graph has 12 edges. What can you now say about the value of d?

3 A graph G is shown on the right.

    a Write down an Eulerian trail, starting at vertex A.

    b Write down a Hamiltonian cycle starting at vertex A.

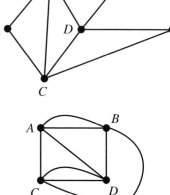

*Questions **4** and **5** are about the graph shown on the right.*

4 **a** Explain why $A - B - C - D - A$ is not an Eulerian trail.

    b Write down the degrees of the vertices and explain how this shows you that the graph is Eulerian.

    c Write down an Eulerian trail for the graph.

5 **a** Explain why $A - B - D - C - A - B - C - D - A$ is not a Hamiltonian cycle for the graph.

    b Write down a Hamiltonian cycle for the graph.

6 **a** Is the graph K_5 Eulerian, semi-Eulerian or neither? Explain how you know.

    b What is the least number of edges that need to be removed from the graph K_4 to make it Eulerian?

7 Ignoring the starting point and the direction of travel, how many distinct Hamiltonian cycles are there on the graph K_4?

8 A simply connected Eulerian graph connects five vertices using six edges. Does a Hamiltonian cycle exist on such a graph?

2.6 Representing networks

Edge weights, distance matrices.

An **edge weight** is a numerical value given to an edge that may represent a distance, a journey time, a profit or a cost, for example.

A **network** is a graph with weighted edges.

A network may be represented as a diagram or by using a **distance matrix**.

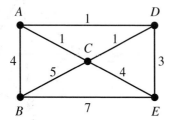

The diagram shows edge weights that represent the distance from one vertex to another.

> **Note:**
> The diagram could equally represent the cost to get from one city to the next – the matrix would then be called a **cost matrix**.

The distance matrix for the network represents the same information as the diagram but in matrix form.

$$\begin{array}{c} \\ A \\ B \\ C \\ D \\ E \end{array} \begin{array}{c} \begin{array}{ccccc} A & B & C & D & E \end{array} \\ \left[\begin{array}{ccccc} - & 4 & 1 & 1 & - \\ 4 & - & 5 & - & 7 \\ 1 & 5 & - & 1 & 4 \\ 1 & - & 1 & - & 3 \\ - & 7 & 4 & 3 & - \end{array} \right] \end{array}$$

Note:

In a distance matrix the numbers represent the edge weights and 0 or '–' means that there is no edge directly joining these two vertices.

Example 2.7 Draw the network represented by this distance matrix:

$$\begin{array}{c} \\ A \\ B \\ C \\ D \\ E \end{array} \begin{array}{c} \begin{array}{ccccc} A & B & C & D & E \end{array} \\ \left[\begin{array}{ccccc} - & 3 & - & 2 & 1 \\ 3 & - & 4 & 2 & - \\ - & 4 & - & - & 5 \\ 2 & 2 & - & - & 3 \\ 1 & - & 5 & 3 & - \end{array} \right] \end{array}$$

Step 1: Draw five vertices labelled A, B, C, D, E.

Step 2: Draw an edge connecting pairs where a value is written and write the weight on the edge.

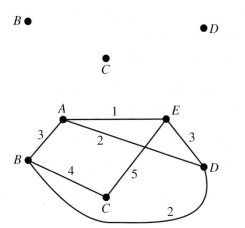

SKILLS CHECK 2E: Representing networks

1 Draw the network represented by this distance matrix:

$$\begin{array}{c} \\ A \\ B \\ C \\ D \end{array} \begin{array}{c} \begin{array}{cccc} A & B & C & D \end{array} \\ \left[\begin{array}{cccc} 0 & 3 & 4 & 1 \\ 3 & 0 & 2 & 3 \\ 4 & 2 & 0 & 2 \\ 1 & 3 & 2 & 0 \end{array} \right] \end{array}$$

2 Write down a distance matrix to represent the network on the right.

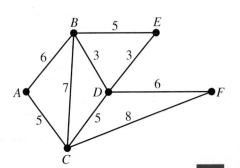

3 Draw the network represented by the distance matrix

$$\begin{array}{c} & \text{To} \\ & \begin{array}{ccc} F & G & H \end{array} \\ \text{From} \begin{array}{c} F \\ G \\ H \end{array} & \left[\begin{array}{ccc} - & 5 & 2 \\ 3 & - & 4 \\ 2 & 4 & - \end{array} \right] \end{array}$$

4 Write down a distance matrix to represent the network below.

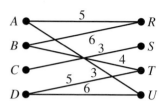

5 Calculate the length of an Eulerian trail on the network represented by the distance matrix

$$\begin{array}{c} & \begin{array}{cccc} A & B & C & D \end{array} \\ \begin{array}{c} A \\ B \\ C \\ D \end{array} & \left[\begin{array}{cccc} - & 2 & 3 & - \\ 2 & - & - & 4 \\ 3 & - & - & 2 \\ - & 4 & 2 & - \end{array} \right] \end{array}$$

6 Annie lives 2 miles from each of Bob, Carl and Dawn. Bob lives 1 mile from Dawn, and Carl lives 3 miles from Dawn.

   a Write down a distance matrix to represent this information.

   b What is the shortest distance between where Bob lives and where Carl lives, according to your matrix?

7 The Hamiltonian cycles in the network represented by the distance matrix below are all of the same length. What is the value of x?

$$\begin{array}{c} & \begin{array}{cccc} A & B & C & D \end{array} \\ \begin{array}{c} A \\ B \\ C \\ D \end{array} & \left[\begin{array}{cccc} - & x & 12 & 15 \\ x & - & 10 & 13 \\ 12 & 10 & - & 18 \\ 15 & 13 & 18 & - \end{array} \right] \end{array}$$

8 The matrix below shows the direct travel times, in minutes, between five underground stations.

$$\begin{array}{c} & \begin{array}{ccccc} P & Q & R & S & T \end{array} \\ \begin{array}{c} P \\ Q \\ R \\ S \\ T \end{array} & \left[\begin{array}{ccccc} - & 8 & 12 & 14 & 20 \\ 8 & - & 7 & 6 & 14 \\ 12 & 7 & - & 10 & 15 \\ 14 & 6 & 10 & - & 18 \\ 20 & 14 & 15 & 18 & - \end{array} \right] \end{array}$$

The time for a journey is found by adding the direct travel times for each leg of the journey and then adding an extra 2 minutes for each station passed through, excluding the start and finish.

   a What is the journey time for a passenger who gets on at P and travels to T via Q?

   b What is the journey time for the quickest Hamiltonian cycle on the network?

2.7 Trees

Trees.

A **tree** is a single, simple graph on which there are no cycles. The following are all examples of trees.

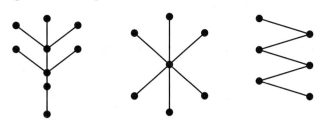

Any graph has a **spanning tree** (a subgraph that connects all the vertices on the original graph, and is also a tree). A spanning tree on a graph with *n* vertices will have *n* − 1 edges.

Original graph   One spanning tree   Another spanning tree

A **minimum spanning tree** is a spanning tree of minimum total weight on a network. It is a spanning tree for which the sum of the edge weights is as small as possible.

A minimum spanning tree can also be called a **minimum connector**.

SKILLS CHECK 2F: Trees

1 A connected graph *G* has *n* vertices. State the number of edges on a spanning tree on *G*.

2 A network has four vertices and four edges. The edge weights are 2, 5, 10 and 20. The minimum spanning tree has weight 32. Draw a diagram to show a network that fits this description.

3 There are only three non-isomorphic spanning trees that can be drawn on five vertices. Draw diagrams to show all three types.

4 a A spanning tree includes a vertex of order 5, explain why it must have at least five vertices of order 1.

b Draw a spanning tree that includes a vertex of order 5 and has exactly six vertices of order 1.

5 Explain why a spanning tree cannot have vertices of orders 1, 1, 1, 1, 2, 3.

6 A network is represented by the matrix below. The minimum spanning tree has weight 35. What can you conclude about the value of *x*?

$$
\begin{array}{c c}
 & \begin{array}{c c c c} A & B & C & D \end{array} \\
\begin{array}{c} A \\ B \\ C \\ D \end{array} &
\left[\begin{array}{c c c c}
- & x & 12 & 15 \\
x & - & 10 & 13 \\
12 & 10 & - & 18 \\
15 & 13 & 18 & -
\end{array} \right]
\end{array}
$$

7 **a** Explain why a tree can never be an Eulerian graph.

  b What is the length of the shortest closed trail through every vertex of a tree?

8 A tree has vertices of degree 1, 1, 1, 2, 3, *n*.

  a How many vertices does the tree have?

  b How many edges does the tree have?

  c Calculate the value of *n*.

Examination practice   Graphs and networks

1 **a** A connected graph has four vertices. State the number of edges in the graph's minimum spanning tree.

  b A graph has *n* vertices. The graph is complete, i.e. each vertex is joined to every other vertex by exactly one edge.

    i State the number of edges in the graph's minimum spanning tree.

    ii Determine the number of Hamiltonian cycles in the graph.

  c A connected graph has four vertices and has arc lengths of

    4, 4.5, 5, 6.5, 7, 8 and 9 units.

    The length of its minimum spanning tree is 17 units. Draw a sketch to show a possible graph.

    [AQA(A) June 2001]

2 The following question refers to the three graphs: **Graph 1**, **Graph 2** and **Graph 3**.

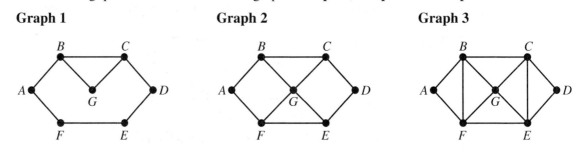

Graph 1   **Graph 2**   **Graph 3**

For **each** of the graphs explain whether or not the graph is Eulerian.   [AQA(A) Jan 2002]

3 A graph *G* has five vertices.

  a **i** Given that *G* is connected, state the number of arcs on a minimum spanning tree.

    ii Given that *G* is Eulerian with all vertices having the same degree *d*, state the minimum value of *d*.

    iii Given that *G* has a Hamiltonian cycle, state the number of edges in such a cycle.

  b Given that *G* has all the properties mentioned in part **a**, draw a possible graph *G*.

    [AQA(A) Jan 2003]

4 a Draw a graph representing this adjacency matrix.

	A	B	C	D	E
A	0	1	0	2	0
B	1	0	2	0	0
C	0	2	0	1	1
D	2	0	1	0	0
E	0	0	1	0	0

b Draw a spanning tree for your graph.

c Construct an adjacency matrix that your spanning tree represents.

5 a Draw a network representing this distance matrix.

	A	B	C	D	E
A	–	4	–	3	–
B	4	–	2	–	–
C	–	2	–	1	6
D	3	–	1	–	2
E	–	–	6	2	–

b Construct an Eulerian trail for your graph, starting at vertex *A*.

c Calculate the length of your Eulerian trail.

6 A simply connected graph has six vertices and nine edges.

a What is the sum of the degrees of the vertices?

b Explain why such a graph cannot have three vertices of degree 5.

c Draw an example of a simply connected Eulerian graph with six vertices and nine edges.

7 A graph *G* is shown.

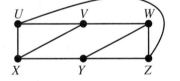

a Explain why $U – X – V – Y – W – Z$ is not a trail on *G*.

b Explain why $U – V – W – Z – U – X – Y$ is not a path on *G*.

c Explain why $U – Z – Y – X – V – U$ is not a Hamiltonian cycle on *G*.

8 A graph has the adjacency matrix

$$
\begin{array}{c}
 \\
A \\ B \\ C \\ D \\ E
\end{array}
\begin{array}{c}
\begin{array}{ccccc} A & B & C & D & E \end{array} \\
\left[
\begin{array}{ccccc}
- & 1 & 1 & 1 & - \\
1 & - & - & 1 & 1 \\
1 & - & - & 1 & - \\
1 & 1 & 1 & - & 1 \\
- & 1 & - & 1 & -
\end{array}
\right]
\end{array}
$$

a Draw a diagram of a graph that could be represented by this adjacency matrix.

b List a Hamiltonian cycle on this graph.

c For this graph, calculate the number of spanning trees that use neither of the edges *AC* and *AD*, explaining your reasoning.

3 Spanning tree problems

A spanning tree on n vertices has $n - 1$ edges. A minimum spanning tree is the one for which the sum of edge weights is as small as possible.

3.1 Greediness

Greediness.

Greediness means 'grabbing whatever is best from the current state without regard to the possible future consequences'.

Greedy algorithms are used to solve problems in which you need an optimum solution. At each stage of such an algorithm, the best choice is made *at the point under consideration*. A greedy algorithm does not go back to reconsider a decision. Kruskal's and Prim's algorithms, explained below, are examples of greedy algorithms. This approach works well for constructing minimum spanning trees.

3.2 Kruskal's and Prim's algorithms

Kruskal's and Prim's algorithms to find minimum spanning trees.
Relative advantages of the two algorithms.

One way to construct a minimum spanning tree for a network is to use **Kruskal's algorithm**.

- List the edges in increasing order of weight.

- Choose the edge with least weight.

- Build a tree by working down the list and choosing connecting edges of least weight, provided they do *not* form a cycle when added to the edges already chosen. (If there are two edges of equal weight, choose either.)

- Stop when no more edges can be chosen.

Another way to construct a minimum spanning tree for a network is by using **Prim's algorithm**.

- Choose a vertex.

- Build a tree by choosing the minimum weight edge that joins a vertex that has not yet been chosen to one that has. Add this edge and the vertex at its end to the tree.

- Repeat this tree-building process until all the vertices have been chosen.

Example 3.1 Use Kruskal's algorithm to construct a minimum spanning tree for the network shown, and give its total weight.

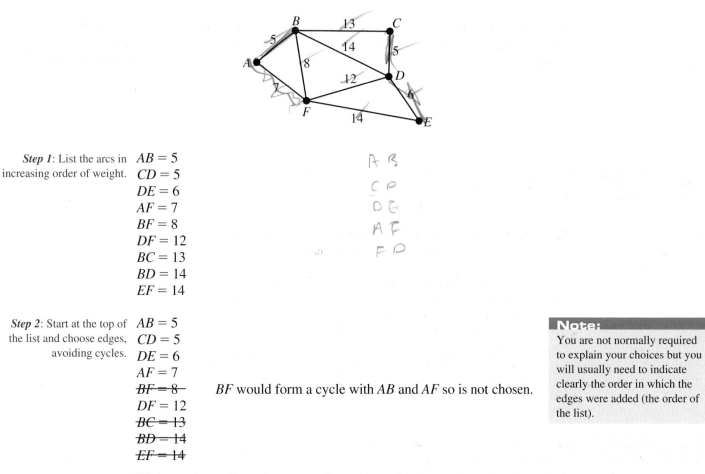

Step 1: List the arcs in increasing order of weight.

$AB = 5$
$CD = 5$
$DE = 6$
$AF = 7$
$BF = 8$
$DF = 12$
$BC = 13$
$BD = 14$
$EF = 14$

Step 2: Start at the top of the list and choose edges, avoiding cycles.

$AB = 5$
$CD = 5$
$DE = 6$
$AF = 7$
~~$BF = 8$~~
$DF = 12$
~~$BC = 13$~~
~~$BD = 14$~~
~~$EF = 14$~~

BF would form a cycle with AB and AF so is not chosen.

Note:
You are not normally required to explain your choices but you will usually need to indicate clearly the order in which the edges were added (the order of the list).

We have chosen five edges so we have a spanning tree.

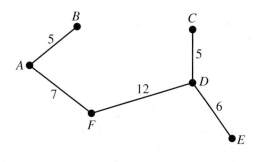

Tip:
Draw the vertices and then add edges as they are chosen.

Note:
It is helpful to draw the tree as it is built. You do not need to draw separate diagrams for each edge added.

Step 3: Calculate the total weight.

Total weight = 35.

Example 3.2 Use Prim's algorithm, starting at vertex A, to build a minimum spanning tree for the network in Example 3.1.

Step 1: Find the minimum weight edge from $\{A\}$ to $\{B, C, D, E, F\}$.

$AB = 5$

Step 2: Find the minimum weight edge joining $\{A, B\}$ to $\{C, D, E, F\}$.

$AF = 7$

Step 3: Find the minimum weight edge joining $\{A, B, F\}$ to $\{C, D, E\}$.

$DF = 12$

Step 4: Find the minimum weight edge joining $\{A, B, D, F\}$ to $\{C, E\}$.

$CD = 5$

Step 5: Find the minimum weight edge joining $\{A, B, C, D, F\}$ to $\{E\}$.

$DE = 6$

Step 6: Draw a diagram to show which edges are in your minimum spanning tree.

Note:
You would not normally need to describe the method in this amount of detail.

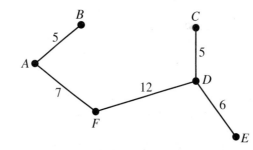

The most important thing to note about Prim's algorithm is that when you look to find the minimum weight edge, look at all the edges between the set of vertices that are in the tree and the set of vertices that are not yet in the tree. Do *not* just build on from the most recent vertex that was added.

Prim's algorithm can also be set up to work on a network represented by a distance matrix.

The matrix formulation of Prim's algorithm is:

- Choose a vertex.
- Circle this vertex in the top row of the matrix and cross out the row corresponding to this vertex. Choose and circle the minimum entry that has not been crossed out in the columns with circled vertices in the top row.
- Choose the vertex for the row of the chosen entry. Note the order in which vertices are chosen.
- Repeat this process until all the vertices have been chosen.

Note:
This exactly mimics the tree-building process. Circling a vertex corresponds to adding it to the set of vertices that are in the tree, and crossing out a row corresponds to deleting a vertex from the set of vertices that are not yet in the tree.

As with the network form of Prim's algorithm, it is important that we look down *all* the columns with circled vertices in the top row at all the entries that are not crossed out to find the minimum. We do *not* just look down the column for the vertex that was most recently chosen.

If the information given about the network is given as a table, then Prim's algorithm is the better method to use.

Example 3.3 Use Prim's algorithm to find a minimum spanning tree for the network with the following distance matrix.

	P	Q	R	S	T	U
P	–	15	31	–	14	–
Q	15	–	10	8	–	20
R	31	10	–	16	–	24
S	–	8	16	–	21	–
T	14	–	–	21	–	12
U	–	20	24	–	12	–

Step 1: Select P, say, as the first vertex. Circle P in the top row, then cross out the P row. Look down the P column to find the minimum entry.

Order of selection

	(P)	Q	R	S	T	U
1	P̶	1̶5̶	3̶1̶	–	1̶4̶	–
	Q	15	–	10	8	–	20
	R	31	10	–	16	–	24
	S	–	8	16	–	21	–
	T	14	–	–	21	–	12
	U	–	20	24	–	12	–

Step 2: Choose the entry 14 in row T. Circle T in the top row and cross out the T row. Look down *both* the P column and the T column to find the minimum entry.

Order of selection

	(P)	Q	R	S	(T)	U
1	P̶	–	1̶5̶	3̶1̶	–	1̶4̶	–
	Q	15	–	10	8	–	20
	R	31	10	–	16	–	24
	S	–	8	16	–	21	–
2	T̶	(14)	–	–	2̶1̶	–	1̶2̶
	U	–	20	24	–	12	–

$PT = 14$

Step 3: Choose the entry 12 in row U. Circle U in the top row and cross out the U row. Look down *all* of the P, T and U columns to find the minimum entry.

Order of selection

	(P)	Q	R	S	(T)	(U)
1	P̶	–	1̶5̶	3̶1̶	–	1̶4̶	–
	Q	15	–	10	8	–	20
	R	31	10	–	16	–	24
	S	–	8	16	–	21	–
2	T̶	(14)	–	–	2̶1̶	–	1̶2̶
3	U̶	–	2̶0̶	2̶4̶	–	(12)	–

$PT = 14$
$TU = 12$

Step 4: Choose the entry 15 in row Q.

Order of selection

	(P)	(Q)	R	S	(T)	(U)
1	P̶	–	1̶5̶	3̶1̶	–	1̶4̶	–
4	Q̶	(15)	–	1̶0̶	8̶	–	2̶0̶
	R	31	10	–	16	–	24
	S	–	8	16	–	21	–
2	T̶	(14)	–	–	2̶1̶	–	1̶2̶
3	U̶	–	2̶0̶	2̶4̶	–	(12)	–

$PT = 14$
$TU = 12$
$PQ = 15$

Step 5: Continue in this way until all vertices have been chosen.

When the algorithm has finished, the answer will look like this:

Order of selection

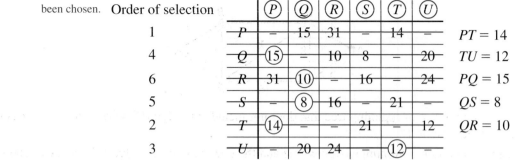

	P	Q	R	S	T	U	
1	P	–	15	31	–	14	–	$PT = 14$
4	Q	(15)	–	10	8	–	20	$TU = 12$
6	R	31	(10)	–	16	–	24	$PQ = 15$
5	S	–	(8)	16	–	21	–	$QS = 8$
2	T	(14)	–	–	21	–	12	$QR = 10$
3	U	–	20	24	–	(12)	–	

SKILLS CHECK **3A: Spanning tree problems**

1 Use Kruskal's algorithm to find the minimum spanning tree for the network below.

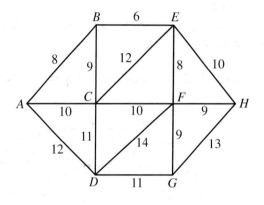

2 Use Prim's algorithm to find the minimum spanning tree for the network shown. Start building your tree from vertex *A*. State the length of your tree.

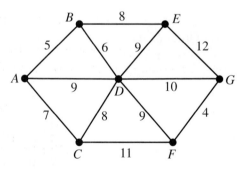

3 Use Prim's algorithm to find the edges in the minimum spanning tree for the network represented by the distance matrix shown. State the order in which edges were added to your tree and give its total length. Draw a diagram to show the edges in your minimum spanning tree.

	A	B	C	D
A	–	12	5	10
B	12	–	11	18
C	5	11	–	11
D	10	18	11	–

4 Prim's algorithm is used to construct a minimum spanning tree for the network shown.

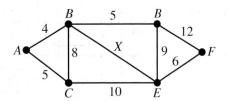

a If there is a minimum spanning tree that does not include the edge *BE*, what is the least possible value of the weight *X*?

b If there is a unique minimum spanning tree and the tree includes the edge *BE*, what can you say about the weight *X*?

5 a By considering what happens when Kruskal's algorithm is applied to a network, formed from a simple graph, in which all the edge weights are different, explain why the two least weight edges in a network must always be included in a minimum spanning tree.

b Draw a diagram to show an example of a network, formed from a simple graph, in which all the edge weights are different, for which the three least weight edges are not all included in the minimum spanning tree.

c Draw a diagram to show an example of a network in which the greatest weight edge is included in the minimum spanning tree.

6 a Use Prim's algorithm to find a minimum spanning tree for the network shown. Start building your tree from vertex *A*.

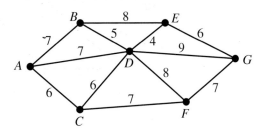

b Find a different minimum spanning tree for the network shown.

7 Use Prim's algorithm to find the edges in a minimum spanning tree for the network represented by the distance matrix below. Start building your tree at vertex *P*.

$$
\begin{array}{c|ccccc}
 & P & Q & R & S & T \\
\hline
P & - & 8 & 12 & 14 & 20 \\
Q & 8 & - & 7 & 6 & 14 \\
R & 12 & 7 & - & 10 & 15 \\
S & 14 & 6 & 10 & - & 18 \\
T & 20 & 14 & 15 & 18 & - \\
\end{array}
$$

8 Kruskal's algorithm is used to construct a minimum spanning tree for the network shown on the right.

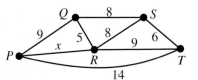

a If the minimum spanning tree must use the edge *PR*, what can be said about *x*?

b If the minimum spanning tree must use the edge *PQ*, what can be said about *x*?

c Which edges must always be included in the minimum spanning tree?

d Which edges can never be included in the minimum spanning tree?

e Between what values does the weight of the minimum spanning tree lie?

1 The following diagram shows the lengths of roads, in miles, connecting eight towns.

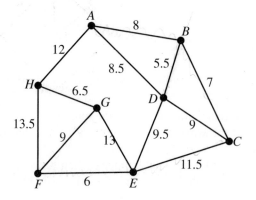

Using Kruskal's algorithm, showing your working at each stage, find the minimum spanning tree for the network. State its length.

[AQA(A) June 2003]

2 The following diagram shows the lengths, in miles, of roads connecting ten towns.

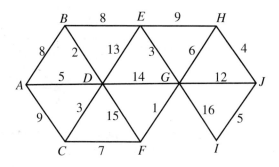

Using Kruskal's algorithm, showing the order in which you select the edges, to find the minimum spanning tree for the network. Draw your minimum spanning tree and state its length.

[AQA(A) June 2003]

3 The following diagram shows a network of roads connecting eight towns. The number on each arc represents the distance, in miles, between two towns.

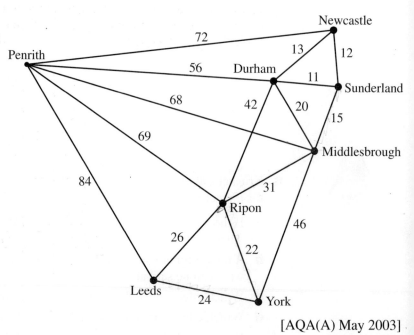

a Starting from Ripon and showing your working at each stage, use Prim's algorithm to find the minimum spanning tree for the eight towns. State the length of your minimum spanning tree.

b Draw your minimum spanning tree.

[AQA(A) May 2003]

4 The following diagram shows the lengths, in km, of tracks connecting seven railway stations.

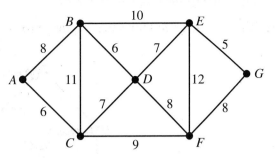

a Use Kruskal's algorithm, showing the order in which you select the edges, to find a minimum spanning tree for the network.

b Draw your minimum spanning tree and state its length.

5 The following diagram shows a network of cables connecting six offices. The value on each edge represents the length of the cable in metres.

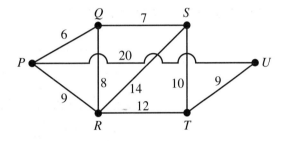

a Use Prim's algorithm, starting from P, to find a minimum spanning tree for the six offices. State the length of your minimum spanning tree.

b An extra cable is added joining Q to T. The length of this cable is x metres. The minimum spanning tree is now of length 35 metres. Calculate the value of x.

6 Use Prim's algorithm, starting at vertex A, to find a minimum spanning tree for the network represented by the distance matrix below. Show the order in which vertices were added to the tree and give its total weight.

	A	B	C	D	E	F	G	H
A	–	6	–	4	–	8	–	5
B	6	–	3	6	5	–	7	7
C	–	3	–	–	6	–	6	–
D	4	6	–	–	–	7	–	–
E	–	5	6	–	–	–	5	–
F	8	–	–	7	–	–	–	4
G	–	7	6	–	5	–	–	2
H	5	7	–	–	–	4	2	–

7 a Apply Prim's algorithm, starting at vertex A, to find a minimum spanning tree for the network represented by the distance matrix below.

	A	B	C	D	E	F
A	–	3	4	5	6	7
B	3	–	2	4	8	9
C	4	2	–	5	7	8
D	5	4	5	–	9	7
E	6	8	7	9	–	6
F	7	9	8	7	6	–

b Draw a diagram to show the edes in your minimum spanning tree.

8 Use Prim's algorithm, starting from V, to find a minimum spanning tree for the network below. Is this the only minimum spanning tree for this network? Explain your answer.

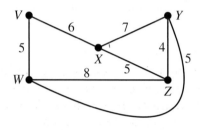

4 Matching

4.1 Representing matching problems graphically using bipartite graphs

Use of bipartite graphs.

Matching problems are based on two subsets of information. Bipartite graphs contain two subsets of vertices and can be used to represent matching problems.

For matching problems draw one set of vertices on the left-hand side and the other set on the right-hand side of the graph. Vertices within each set are usually placed in a vertical line.

Edges can then be used to show possible pairings between elements of the two sets.

> **Recall:**
> A bipartite graph is a graph with two sets of vertices such that edges only connect vertices from one set to vertices in the other set, and there are no edges connecting vertices within either set.

Example 4.1 Alex, Bill, Carol and Dalbit have applied for some jobs. The jobs are electrician, firefighter, groundskeeper and housekeeper. Alex has applied to be the electrician or the groundskeeper; Bill has applied to be the electrician or the firefighter; Carol has applied to be the firefighter, the groundskeeper or the housekeeper; Dalbit has applied to be the groundskeeper.

Draw a bipartite graph to represent this information.

Step 1: Draw a column of vertices for *A*, *B*, *C* and *D* and draw a column of vertices for *E*, *F*, *G* and *H*.

Step 2: Draw edges to connect the people to the jobs they have applied for.

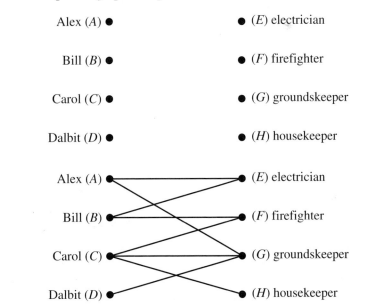

A **matching** is a set of edges in the bipartite graph with no vertices in common. For a **complete matching**, the left-hand set and the right-hand set must both have the same number of elements and this is also the number of edges in the matching. If any element is not joined to an edge, the matching is incomplete.

A **maximal matching** is a one for which there is no matching on the bipartite graph that uses a greater number of edges. A complete matching is always maximal but sometimes there is no complete matching and we would want to find the maximal incomplete matching.

Example 4.2 Draw bipartite graphs to illustrate each of the following and say whether or not they are a matching. For those that are a matching, say whether or not they are a complete matching.

a Give Alex the job of electrician, Bill the job of firefighter and Carol the job of groundskeeper.

b Give Alex the job of electrician, Bill the job of firefighter and give Carol and Dalbit the job of groundskeeper.

c Give Alex the job of electrician, Bill the job of firefighter, Carol the job of housekeeper and Dalbit the job of groundskeeper.

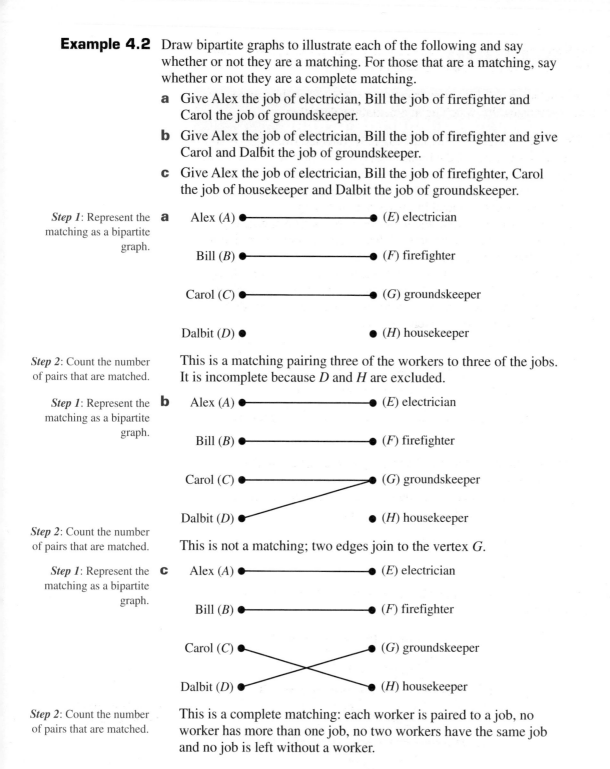

Step 1: Represent the matching as a bipartite graph.

a

Alex (*A*) ● ———————— ● (*E*) electrician

Bill (*B*) ● ———————— ● (*F*) firefighter

Carol (*C*) ● ———————— ● (*G*) groundskeeper

Dalbit (*D*) ●   ● (*H*) housekeeper

Step 2: Count the number of pairs that are matched.

This is a matching pairing three of the workers to three of the jobs. It is incomplete because *D* and *H* are excluded.

Step 1: Represent the matching as a bipartite graph.

b

Alex (*A*) ● ———————— ● (*E*) electrician

Bill (*B*) ● ———————— ● (*F*) firefighter

Carol (*C*) ● ———————— ● (*G*) groundskeeper

Dalbit (*D*) ●   ● (*H*) housekeeper

Step 2: Count the number of pairs that are matched.

This is not a matching; two edges join to the vertex *G*.

Step 1: Represent the matching as a bipartite graph.

c

Alex (*A*) ● ———————— ● (*E*) electrician

Bill (*B*) ● ———————— ● (*F*) firefighter

Carol (*C*) ●   ● (*G*) groundskeeper

Dalbit (*D*) ●   ● (*H*) housekeeper

Step 2: Count the number of pairs that are matched.

This is a complete matching: each worker is paired to a job, no worker has more than one job, no two workers have the same job and no job is left without a worker.

4.2 Improving matching

Improvement of matching using an algorithm.

For the bipartite graph in Example 4.1, just using common sense you can see that, since Dalbit has only applied for the job of groundskeeper and Carol is the only worker who has applied for the job of housekeeper, any complete matching must pair *D* with *G* and *C* with *H*. It is then easy to see that the only complete matching is that shown in Example 4.2**c**.

For larger problems, you cannot rely on common sense; a systematic method for finding a maximal matching is needed.

The usual approach is to start from any matching and then try to improve it using the matching augmentation algorithm.

- Consider all edges of the matching to be directed from right to left and all other edges of the bipartite graph to be directed from left to right.
- Create a new vertex X joined with directed edges to each left-hand vertex that is not included in the current matching.
- Start from X and move to the left-hand vertices then alternately move between right-hand and left-hand vertices, only ever visiting vertices that have not been visited already.
- If a right-hand vertex that is not included in the current matching is reached then a breakthrough has been made; if it is impossible to add any more edges without visiting a vertex that has already been visited then the current matching is maximal.
- If a breakthrough occurs we can construct an alternating path from X to the right-hand vertex reached and use this to augment the current matching to get an improved matching. Unless this is now a maximal matching, we then run the algorithm again.

Having found an alternating path, augment the current matching as follows:

- remove from the current matching any edges that are in the alternating path
- add to the current matching any edges that are in the alternating path but were not in the current matching.

This gives the improved matching.

Example 4.3 Apply the matching augmentation algorithm to the matching in Example 4.2**a**.

Step 1: Draw the bipartite graph and add a vertex X joined to D.

Step 2: Mark the edges in the matching with arrows pointing to the left and the other edges of the bipartite graph with arrows pointing to the right.

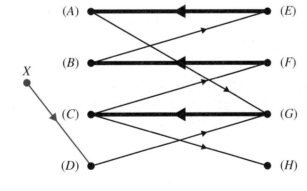

Note:
You are trying to get a breakthrough to H.

Note:
If there is more than one alternating path that makes a breakthrough, choose the shortest.

Step 3: Construct an alternating path from X to H. $X - D - G - C - H$

Step 4: Augment the incomplete matching using the alternating path.

Remove $C - G$ from the current matching; add $D - G$, $C - H$.

The maximal matching is $A - E$, $B - F$, $C - H$, $D - G$.

Formally, we assign each edge a weight of 1 and use an algorithm to find the shortest alternating path from X to a right-hand vertex that was not included in the matching that we started with. We need the vertex X so that the paths all have a common starting point.

You can also represent the bipartite graph using an adjacency matrix, by making the left-hand vertices the row labels and the right-hand vertices the column labels. Every entry in the matrix is either a 0 or a 1 and you need to find the maximum number of 1s such that no two of them are in the same row and no two of them are in the same column.

1 The matrix shows the availability of four workers A, B, C and D to complete four tasks 1, 2, 3 and 4.

	1	2	3	4
A	1	0	0	1
B	0	1	1	0
C	1	1	0	0
D	0	1	1	0

Represent this information as a bipartite graph.

2 The matrix shows the availability of four workers A, B, C and D to complete four tasks 1, 2, 3 and 4.

	1	2	3	4
A	1	0	0	1
B	0	1	1	0
C	1	1	0	0
D	0	1	1	0

Initially worker A is assigned to task 1, worker B to task 2 and worker D to task 3. By using an algorithm from this initial matching, show how each worker can be assigned to a task for which they are available.

3 Now consider the matrix in question **1** but suppose that worker D is not available for task 3 after all. Initially worker A is assigned to task 1 and worker B to task 2. Construct an alternating path to match three workers to tasks. Use a further alternating path, or paths, to find a complete matching.

4 Five children have been asked for their first and second choices for which pet they will take home from school for the weekend. The pupils cannot share a pet.

Pupil	First choice	Second choice
Adam	Freddy the frog	Rupert the rabbit
Bruno	Gareth the gerbil	Hamish the hamster
Cassandra	Rupert the rabbit	Hamish the hamster
Diana	Freddy the frog	Gareth the gerbil
Elizabeth	Hamish the hamster	Simon the snake

a Show this information on a bipartite graph, using A, B, C, D and E for the five children and F, G, H, R, S for the five pets, in that order.

The teacher initially says that Adam can take Freddy the frog, Bruno can take Gareth the gerbil, Cassandra can take Rupert the rabbit and Elizabeth can take Hamish the hamster.

b Show this incomplete matching on a bipartite graph and use an algorithm to construct an alternating path. Hence construct a complete matching between the children and the pets.

c How many children have their first choice of pet?

5 Adam, Briony, Charlie, Debbie and Ed are choosing what they want for lunch from a menu. Adam wants pie or tuna; Briony wants salad or tuna; Charlie wants pie or quiche; Debbie wants quiche or salad; and Ed wants ravioli or salad.

a Represent this information as a bipartite graph.

Adam and Charlie both choose pie, Briony chooses tuna, Debbie chooses quiche and Ed chooses salad. The waitress then realises that there is only one portion of each meal left, so Adam and Charlie cannot both have pie.

b Construct an alternating path to find a complete matching between the five people and the five meals.

6 The bipartite graph shows which of five workers *R*, *S*, *T*, *U* and *W* are able to undertake which of five tasks 1, 2, 3, 4 and 5. Each task is to be done by one worker and each worker is to undertake one task.

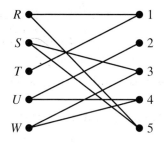

Initially, *R* is assigned task 1, *S* is assigned task 3 and *U* is assigned task 4.

Construct alternating paths to find a complete matching.

7 Alice (*A*), Ben (*B*), Cassie (*C*), Drew (*D*), Euan (*E*) and Fizz (*F*) need to tidy their house. There are six areas to be tidied and they will each tidy one area. The six areas are the boys' bedroom (1), the girls' bedroom (2), the kitchen (3), the bathroom (4), the garage (5) and the garden (6).

Alice, Cassie and Fizz do not want to tidy the boys' bedroom. Additionally, Alice does not want to tidy the garage or the garden, Cassie does not want to tidy the bathroom or the garden and Fizz does not want to tidy the kitchen or the garage.

Ben, Drew and Euan do not want to tidy the bathroom or the kitchen. Additionally, Ben does not want to tidy the girls' bedroom or the garage, Drew does not want to tidy the garden or the boys' bedroom and Euan does not want to tidy the garden or the girls' bedroom.

Draw a bipartite graph showing which areas each person does not want to tidy.

8 a For the situation described in question **7** above, draw a bipartite graph showing who is prepared to tidy which area.

Alice says that she will tidy the bathroom, Cassie will tidy the garage, Fizz will tidy the girls' bedroom and Ben can tidy the boys' bedroom.

b Construct an alternating path to find an improved matching between five of the people and five of the areas to be tidied.

c From this improved matching, construct a second alternating path to find a complete matching.

d Write down a different complete matching between the people and the areas.

1 A group of five pupils have to colour in some pictures. There are five coloured crayons available, Orange (*O*), Red (*R*), Yellow (*Y*), Green (*G*) and Purple (*P*). The five pupils have each told their teacher their first and second choice of coloured crayons.

Pupil	First choice	Second choice
Alison (*A*)	Orange	Yellow
Brian (*B*)	Orange	Red
Carly (*C*)	Yellow	Purple
Danny (*D*)	Red	Purple
Emma (*E*)	Purple	Green

  a Show this information on a bipartite graph.

  b Initially the teacher gives pupils *A*, *C*, *D* and *E* their first choice of crayons. Demonstrate, by using an algorithm from this initial matching, how the teacher can give each pupil either their first or second choice of coloured crayons.

[AQA(A) Jan 2001]

2 a A group of five students are applying to five different universities. The students wish to visit the universities on 14th October but their teacher insists that no more than one student be allowed to visit the same university on that day. They list the two universities that they would like to visit.

Student	First choice	Second choice
Andrew (*A*)	Cambridge	Leeds
Joanne (*J*)	Cambridge	Durham
Rick (*R*)	Leeds	Bristol
Sarah (*S*)	Durham	Bristol
Tom (*T*)	Bristol	Oxford

  i Draw a bipartite graph linking the students to their chosen two universities.

  ii Initially the teacher gives Andrew, Rick, Sarah and Tom their first choices of university.
  Demonstrate, by using an algorithm from this initial matching, how the teacher can allocate each pupil to attend their first or second choice of university.

[AQA(A) Nov 2002]

3 a Draw a bipartite graph representing the following adjacency matrix.

	1	2	3	4	5
A	1	0	1	0	0
B	0	0	1	1	0
C	0	1	0	1	0
D	0	0	1	1	0
E	1	1	0	0	1

  b Given that initially *A* is matched to 3, *B* is matched to 4 and *E* is matched to 1, use the maximum matching algorithm, from this initial matching, to find a complete matching. List your complete matching.

[AQA(A) May 2003]

4 The following adjacency matrix shows which of five students A, B, C, D and E have applied for which of five scholarships 1, 2, 3, 4 and 5. The students are to be matched to the scholarships, one student to each scholarship.

	1	2	3	4	5
A	1	0	1	0	1
B	1	1	0	0	0
C	0	0	1	1	1
D	0	1	0	0	0
E	0	0	0	0	1

a Represent this information on a bipartite graph.

b Initially, student A is awarded scholarship 1, student B is awarded scholarship 2, student C is awarded scholarship 3 and student E is awarded scholarship 5.

Demonstrate, by using an algorithm from this initial matching, how each student can be assigned to a scholarship for which they have applied.

5 Four gymnasts are training for a competition. Only one gymnast can train on each piece of equipment at a time.

Alan wants to use either the floor mat or the parallel bars; Boris wants to use the horse or the rings; Carl wants to use the rings or the floor mat and Derek wants to use the floor mat or the horse.

a Represent this information on a bipartite graph.

Alan arrives first and starts on the floor mat, Boris arrives next and starts on the horse, Carl arrives third and starts on the rings. When Derek arrives he is left with the parallel bars, which was not one of the pieces of equipment that he wanted to use.

b Demonstrate, by using an algorithm from this initial matching, how each gymnast can be assigned to a piece of equipment that they want to use.

c Find a different complete matching between the gymnasts and the pieces of equipment.

6 Four children are choosing from a menu at a burger bar.

Ryan wants either a bacon burger or a cheeseburger, Sam wants either a cheeseburger or a double burger, Tom wants a bacon burger or an egg burger and Will wants either a cheeseburger or an egg burger.

a Represent this information on a bipartite graph.

b The children order one burger of each type. Ryan takes the bacon burger, Sam takes the cheeseburger and Tom takes the egg burger. Will does not want the double burger.

Use an algorithm from this initial matching to show which child should have which burger for them each to have a burger that they wanted.

c Give another matching between the children and the burgers.

d Which of your two matchings involves the fewest swaps between the burgers the children took and the ones they end up with?

5 Shortest paths

5.1 Shortest paths in networks

A shortest path between two vertices on a network is a path with these two vertices as its end points that has the minimum possible total weight. Usually there will be several possible paths with the vertices as the end points, and each path has a weight (the sum of all the weights of the edges that make up the path). We want to find a path for which the weight takes its minimum value.

5.2 Dijkstra's algorithm

Dijkstra's algorithm.

The algorithm for finding a shortest path between two given vertices in an undirected network uses temporary and permanent labels at the vertices. We put a circle round a label to show that it has become permanent.

Begin by labelling the start vertex 0 and making this permanent, then proceed as follows.

- Denote the vertex that has just been given a permanent label by V and the value of the permanent label at V by P.
- Work from V to each vertex that is directly joined to V by an edge. If the new vertex already has a permanent label do nothing, but if not then calculate P + edge weight from V. If this is smaller than any current temporary label at that vertex record it; otherwise leave the current temporary label unchanged.
- When all vertices directly joined to V have been considered, look at the temporary labels at all the vertices that do not have permanent labels, find the smallest and make it permanent. If there is a choice choose any one.
- If all vertices have permanent labels, stop; otherwise go back to the first bullet point.

The permanent labels tell us the length of the shortest path from the start vertex to each labelled vertex. Tracing back through the permanent labels gives the route of any required shortest path.

Example 5.1 Apply Dijkstra's algorithm to find the length of the shortest path from A to F in the network below. The weights on the arcs represent distances in kilometres.

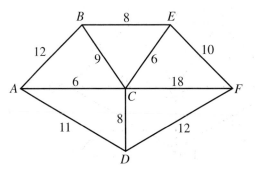

Step 1: Start by giving *A* the permanent label 0.

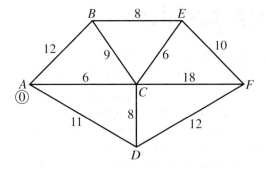

Step 2: Working from *A*, calculate the temporary labels of 12 at *B*, 6 at *C* and 11 at *D*. The smallest temporary label is 6 at *C*, so this becomes permanent.

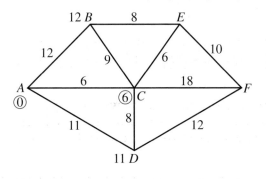

Step 3: Working from *C*, calculate temporary labels of 6 + 6 = 12 at *E* and 6 + 18 = 24 at *F*. The smallest temporary label is 11 at *D*, so this becomes permanent.

Note:

The temporary labels at *B* and *D* are unchanged because 6 + 9 > 12 and 6 + 8 > 11.

Step 4: Working from *D*, change the temporary label at *F* to 11 + 12 = 23. The smallest temporary label is 12 at *B* or *E*; arbitrarily choose to make *B* permanent next.

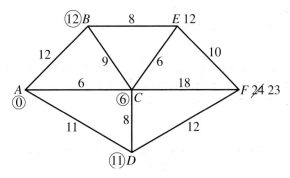

Step 5: Working from *B*, no temporary labels are changed. Make *E* permanent.

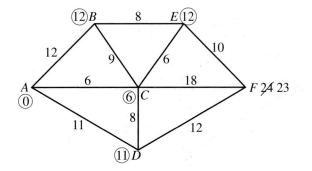

Step 6: Working from *E*, change the temporary label at *F* to 12 + 10 = 22. Make *F* permanent.

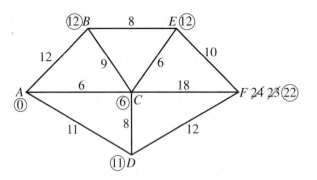

Note:
You only need to show the working on a diagram; there is no need to write an explanation of what has been done.

The working would be shown on a single diagram:

The shortest path from *A* to *F* is of length 22 km.

The permanent labels indicate the length of the shortest path from *A* to each of the other vertices. Use these values to trace back through the network and find the route of the shortest path.

In Example 5.1, the shortest path from *A* to *F* is of length 22 km. Tracing back from *F* indicates that we must have reached *F* via *E*.

$$C: \ 22 - 18 \neq 6$$
$$D: \ 22 - 12 \neq 11$$
$$E: \ 22 - 10 = 12$$

Similarly *E* was reached via *C*, and *C* was reached directly from *A*.

The route of the shortest path is $A - C - E - F$.

Sometimes you may be required to comment on the solution or amend it to take account of the context of the problem. For example, the quickest route may not be the shortest route since the speeds may be different on different types of road.

Note:
You do not need to keep a record of how each permanent label was achieved.

Note:
You would not be expected to use Dijkstra's algorithm on networks with directed edges or negative weights.

SKILLS CHECK **5A: Shortest paths**

*Questions **1**, **2** and **3** refer to the network below.*
This shows the time, in hours, to travel by car between seven towns.

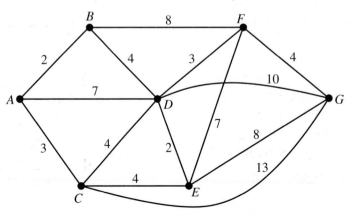

1 a Use Dijkstra's algorithm to find the minimum time to travel from A to G, and state the route that should be taken.

b Give two reasons why the journey time is likely to be longer than this.

2 The traffic report on the radio announces that the road between F and G cannot be used. Use your answer to question **1** to find the minimum time to travel from A to G without using the edge FG.

3 On a different day, the road between F and G is open but one of the other roads is closed. This means that the minimum time is longer than that in question **1** but shorter than that in question **2**. There are three different routes with the new minimum journey time. Which road is closed?

*Questions **4** and **5** refer to the network on the right.*
This shows the distances, in miles, between seven towns.

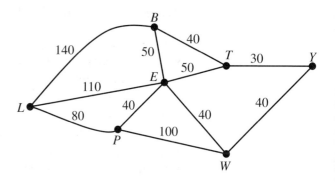

4 Use Dijkstra's algorithm to find the length of the shortest route from L to each of the other towns.

5 On the roads PE and ET, drivers can average 60 miles per hour.
On roads BT, EW and WY, drivers can average 40 miles per hour.
For the first 60 miles of the road from L to E drivers can average 30 miles per hour but the remaining 50 miles can be driven at an average speed of 50 miles per hour.
All the other roads can only be driven at an average speed of 30 miles per hour.

a Copy the network but mark the edges with journey times in minutes.

b Use Dijkstra's algorithm to find the quickest route from L to Y.

6 a Apply Dijkstra's algorithm to the following network, starting from vertex A.

b Find the least weight route from A to each of the other vertices.

c The edge AC gets blocked off and cannot be used. What is the new least weight route from A to G?

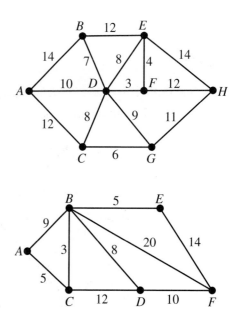

7 The diagram shows a network of roads. The number on each edge is the time, in minutes, to travel along the road.

a Use Dijkstra's algorithm to find the minimum travelling time from A to F.

b State the corresponding route.

8 The diagram shows a network of roads. The number on each edge is the length, in km, of the road.

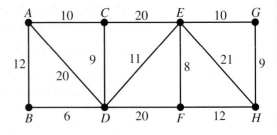

  a Use Dijkstra's algorithm to find the shortest distance from *A* to *H*.

  b State the corresponding route.

  c On a particular day the road *DE* is blocked and cannot be used. Find the new minimum distance from *A* to *H*.

9 The diagram shows a network of roads. The number on each edge is the length, in km, of the road.

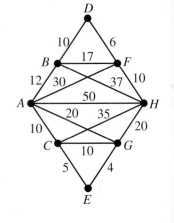

  a Use Dijkstra's algorithm to find the shortest distance from *A* to *H*.

  b State the corresponding route.

  c Find the shortest disance from *D* to *G*.

10 The diagram shows a network of roads. The number on each edge is the length, in km, of the road.

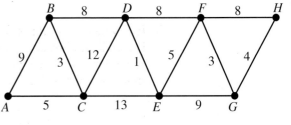

  a Use Dijkstra's algorithm to find the shortest distance from *A* to *H*.

  b State the route corresponding to this minimum distance.

  c A new road of length *x* km, is built connecting *C* to *F*. The minimum distance from *A* to *H* is reduced by using this new road. Find an inequality for *x*.

Examination practice   Shortest paths

1 The following network shows the time, in minutes, to travel between ten towns.

  a Use Dijkstra's algorithm to find the minimum time to travel from *A* to *J*, and state the route.

  b A new road is to be constructed connecting *D* to *E*. Find the time needed for travelling this section of road if the overall minimum journey time to travel from *A* to *J* is reduced by 10 minutes. State the new route.

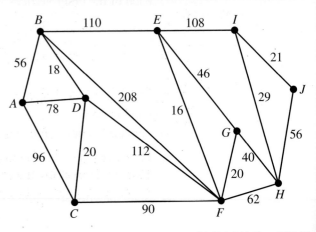

[AQA(A) Jan 2001]

2 Three boys, John, Lee and Safraz, are to take part in a running race.
They are each starting from a different point but they all must finish at the same point *N*.

John starts from the point *A*, Lee from the point *B* and Safraz from the point *C*.

The following diagram shows the network of streets that they may run along.
The numbers on the arcs represent the time, in seconds, taken to run along each street.

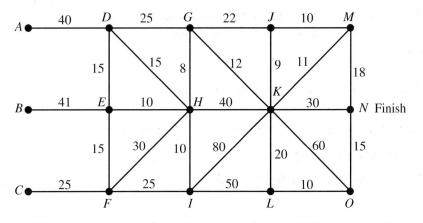

a Working backwards from *N*, or otherwise, use Dijkstra's algorithm to find
the time taken for each of the three boys to complete the course.
Show all your working at each vertex.

b Write down the route that each boy should take. [AQA(A) Nov 2002]

3 Every day, Mary thinks of a rumour to spread on her way to school. The rumour
is then spread from one person to another. The following network shows the
route through which the rumour spreads. The number on each arc represents the
time, in minutes, for the rumour to spread from one person to another.

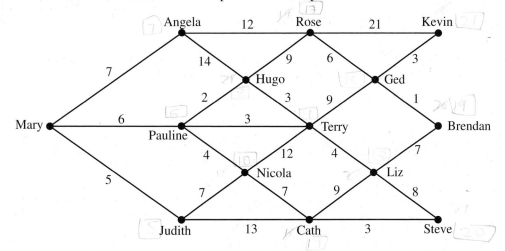

a Use Dijkstra's algorithm to find the time taken for the rumour to reach
each person.

b List the route through which Brendan first hears the rumour.

c On a particular day Pauline is not at school.
Find, by inspection, the extra time that elapses before Brendan first
hears the rumour for that day. [AQA(A) May 2003]

4 The following diagram shows the times, in minutes, taken to drive between eight towns.

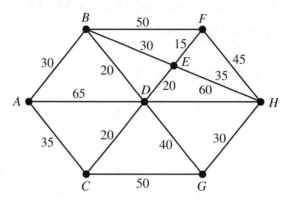

Use Dijkstra's algorithm to find the quickest time to travel from *A* to *H*.
State the route corresponding to this minimum time.

5 The following distance matrix represents a network of roads connecting five villages.
The distances are in miles.

	A	B	C	D	E
A	–	6	–	7	–
B	6	–	8	–	2x
C	–	8	–	5	x
D	7	–	5	–	2x
E	–	2x	x	2x	–

The distances from *E* are unknown, but it is known that the distance from *E* to *B* is the same as the distance from *E* to *D* and that these are each twice as long as the distance from *E* to *C*.

a Draw the network.

b Use Dijkstra's algorithm to find the two possible lengths of the shortest route from *A* to *E*.

c For what values of *x* does the shortest route from *A* to *E* have to pass through *C*?

6 The following diagram shows a network of footpaths connecting six houses. The weights on the edges are the lengths of the footpaths in hundreds of metres.

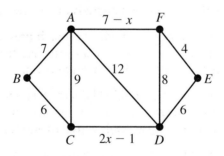

a The direct route from *A* to *D* is shorter than either of the routes *A* – *F* – *D* or *A* – *C* – *D*.
What does this tell you about the value of *x*?

b Dijkstra's algorithm is used to find the shortest distance (in hundreds of metres) from *A* to each of the other houses. Which is the next vertex after *A* where the label becomes permanent, and what can you say about the value of this permanent label?

c Explain why the label at *E* is made permanent before the label at *C*.

6 Route inspection problem

Chinese Postman problem.

The **route inspection problem**, or **Chinese Postman problem**, involves finding the shortest closed trail that covers every edge of a network at least once. This type of problem arises in contexts such as a rail safety expert needing to inspect every piece of track in a railway system or a postman needing to walk along every street to deliver mail in the most efficient way possible.

These contexts can be represented in graph form. If the graph is Eulerian then an Eulerian trail covers every edge exactly once and finishes where it started. This is a solution to the route inspection problem.

If the graph is not Eulerian some edges will have to be covered twice. The Chinese Postman algorithm shows which edges need to be repeated to give a shortest closed trail that covers every edge.

Sometimes the context of the problem means that the trail does not need to start and end at the same vertex. If the start and finish vertices are the only odd vertices then there is a semi-Eulerian trail that covers every edge exactly once. If they are not, the Chinese Postman algorithm can be adapted to find which edges need to be repeated to give a shortest trail covering every edge with the required start and finish vertices.

Chinese Postman algorithm

Start by identifying the vertices of odd degree. In an exam question the number of vertices of odd degree will be 0, 2 or 4; for a practical problem there could be hundreds of vertices of odd degree.

Note:
There is always an even number of vertices of odd degree – this is because each edge has two ends so the sum of the degrees must be even.

When a path passes through a vertex, it uses up two edges: one to come in and one to come out, so with vertices of odd degree we need to repeat an edge to make the degree even.

If there are no vertices of odd degree then the graph is Eulerian and the length of the shortest closed trail that covers every edge is the sum of all the edge weights. In this case a suitable route can easily be found.

If there are two or four vertices of odd degree some edges will need to be repeated. With two vertices of odd degree, pair them in the shortest way possible (i.e. to give the smallest sum of weights). This effectively makes all the vertices have even degree. Add this to the sum of the weights in the complete network.

Note:
In theory you would use Dijkstra's algorithm to find the lengths of the shortest paths joining the vertices of odd degree; in practice you can usually just use common sense for simple problems.

With four vertices of odd degree consider all the different ways in which the odd vertices could be paired (with *all* the vertices of odd degree included) and find the pairing for which the sum of the weights is least. Add this to the sum of the weights.

Example 6.1 **a** Find the length of the shortest closed trail that covers every edge on the network below. The weights on the arcs represent distances in kilometres.

b Write down a suitable route for the network on the right.

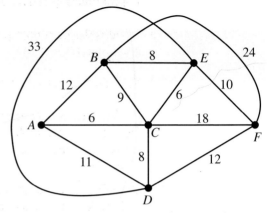

Step 1: Identify the odd vertices.

a The only vertices of odd degree are *A* and *C*.

Step 2: Find the shortest way to pair the odd vertices.

The shortest way to join *A* and *C* is to use the arc *AC* = 6.

Step 3: Find the sum of the weights of the network and add the weight of the shortest pairing.

The sum of all the weights in the network is 157 km. Add to this the length of the repeated edge. The shortest closed trail that uses every edge at least once has length 157 + 6 = 163 km.

Step 4: Write down a suitable route.

b The route must use each arc once, except *AC*, which must occur twice.
For example, *A – B – E – F – D – A – C – B – F – C – E – D – C – A*.

Example 6.2 Find a solution to the route inspection problem on the network on the right.

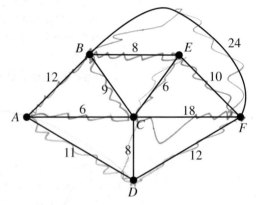

Step 1: Identify the odd vertices.

Vertices *A*, *C*, *D* and *E* have odd degree.

Step 2: Find the shortest path between each pair of odd vertices.

The minimum weights of the connecting paths are:

$AC = 6$, $AD = 11$, $AE = 12$, $CD = 8$,
$CE = 6$, $DE = 14$

Step 3: Pair the odd vertices and calculate the total weight of each pairing.

The possible pairs, in which all the vertices of odd degree are included, are:

AC and $DE = 6 + 14 = 20$
AD and $CE = 11 + 6 = 17$
AE and $CD = 12 + 8 = 20$

Step 4: Identify the least-weight pairing.

The pairing of least weight is AD and $CE = 11 + 6 = 17$.

Step 5: Add the least-weight pairing to the sum of the weights in the network.

The total sum of the weights is 124. Repeat *AD* and *CE* to give a total weight of 141.

Step 6: Write down a suitable route.

A suitable route is: $A – B – E – F – D – A – C – B – F – C – E – C – D – A$.

Note:
The route uses every edge in the network once and repeats *AD* and *CE*.

SKILLS CHECK **6A: Route inspection problem**

Questions **1**, **2** *and* **3** *refer to the network on the right. This shows the time, in hours, to travel by car between seven towns.*

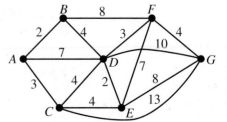

1 Explain why it is not possible to start at *A*, travel along each road exactly once and return to *A*.

2 Find a route around the network that starts at *A*, travels each road at least once and returns to *A* with the minimum journey time. State this minimum journey time.

3 What is the minimum journey time for travelling around the network, starting at *A* and travelling each road at least once, but not necessarily finishing at *A*? Where does such a route end?

4 A connected network has eight odd nodes. In how many ways can these odd nodes be paired?

5 The network on the right shows the corridors linking six classrooms and their lengths, in metres.

   A teacher wants to start at *A* and walk along each corridor at least once before returning to *A*. Calculate the minimum distance that the teacher must walk.

6 **a** Apply the route inspection algorithm to the network on the right to find the weight of the least-weight route that uses every edge on the network, starting at *A* and ending at *H*.

   b Give an example of such a route.

Questions 7 and 8 refer to the diagram on the right, which shows a network of roads. The number on each edge is the length, in km, of the road.

7 **a** Find the length of an optimal 'Chinese postman' route for the network.

   b State a possible corresponding route.

8 **a** A worker starts from *B* and travels along each road at least once before finishing at *E*. Find the length of an optimal route for the worker.

   b State a possible corresponding route.

9 The diagram shows a network of roads. The number on each edge is the length, in km, of the road.

   a Explain why it is not possible to start from *A*, travel along each road only once and return to *A*.

   b Find the length of an optimal 'Chinese postman' route around the network, starting and finishing at *A*.

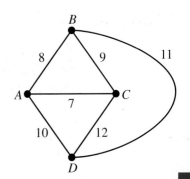

10 For each of the following diagrams state the minimum number of edges that need to be added to make the graph Eulerian and draw your new graph.

a

b

c

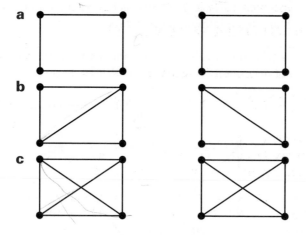

1 The following network shows the time, in minutes, to travel between ten towns.

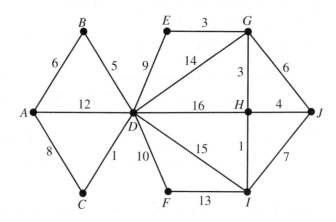

a An ambulance is based at *A* and has to respond to an emergency at *J*. Use Dijkstra's algorithm to find the minimum distance to travel from *A* to *J*, and state the route.

b A police motorcyclist, based at town *A*, has to travel along each of the roads at least once before returning to base at *A*. Find the minimum total distance the motorcyclist must travel.   [AQA(A) May 2002]

2 The diagram on the right shows the paths in St. Stephen's Green, Dublin. The paths *AB* and *CD* are parallel and are each 100 metres long. The perpendicular distance between them is also 100 metres. The point *O* is equidistant from *A*, *B*, *C* and *D*. The path *IJKL* is a circle, centre *O*, of radius 20 metres, and the path *EFGH* is a circle, centre *O*, of radius 40 metres.

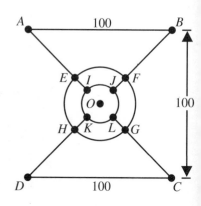

A person enters the park at *A* and is to walk along each path at least once before returning to *A*.

a Giving each answer to the nearest metre, calculate the lengths of the paths:

   i *IJ*;   **ii** *EF*;   **iii** *AE*.

b Calculate the length of an optimal Chinese Postman tour.

c Use Dijkstra's algorithm to find the shortest distance from *A* to *C*. State the **two** routes corresponding to this shortest distance.   [AQA(A) Jan 2003]

3 The diagram on the right shows a network of roads connecting five villages. The numbers on the roads are the times, in minutes, taken to travel along each road, where $x > 0.5$.

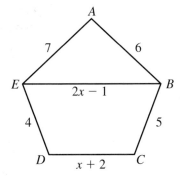

A police patrol car has to travel from its base at B along each road at least once and return to base.

  a Explain why a route from B to E must be repeated.

  b List the routes, and their lengths, from B to E, in terms of x where appropriate.

  c On a particular day, it is known that $x = 10$.
  Find the length of an optimal Chinese Postman route on this day.
  State a possible route corresponding to this minimum length.

  d Find, no matter what the value of x, which of the three routes should **not** be used if the total length of a Chinese Postman route is to be optimal.   [AQA(A) Nov 2003]

4 The following diagram shows the tracks on a small railway network. The vertices represent stations and the distances are in miles.
The route from A to C is a scenic route through a long and winding valley.

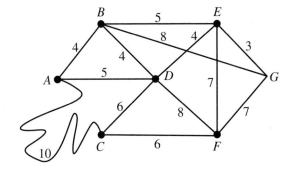

A track inspector wants to check each section of track on the network.
He will start from A, travel each piece of track at least once and return to A. He wants to repeat as short a distance of track as possible.

  a Use the Chinese Postman algorithm to find the minimum length of track that must be repeated.

  b Which pieces of track are travelled twice with this route?

5 The following distance matrix represents a network of roads connecting five villages.
The distances are in miles.

	A	B	C	D	E
A	–	6	–	7	–
B	6	–	8	–	$2x$
C	–	8	–	5	x
D	7	–	5	–	$2x$
E	–	$2x$	x	$2x$	–

The distances from E are unknown, but it is known that the distance from E to B is the same as the distance from E to D and that these are each twice as long as the distance from E to C.

  a Draw the network.

  b Find the length of an optimal Chinese Postman route in the case when $x = 3$.

  c Find the length of an optimal Chinese Postman route in the cases when $x > 8$.

6 The following diagram shows a network of footpaths connecting six houses. The weights on the edges are the lengths of the footpaths in hundreds of metres.

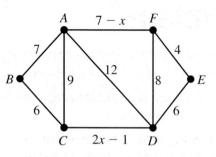

A man walking his dog decides to walk along each footpath at least once, starting and ending at A.

a Explain why the man will need to walk along some of the footpaths twice.

b Explain why, no matter what the value of x is, the man must walk more than 6650 metres.

7 Travelling Salesperson problem

7.1 Practical problems and the classical problem

Finding a tour in a practical problem.

The **Travelling Salesperson problem** requires a minimum tour that visits every vertex of a complete network.

This type of problem might be used to represent a rail inspector who needs to visit every station in a network, as efficiently as possible, to check that the signals are working, returning to the first station.

Recall:
A tour (or cycle) that visits every vertex exactly once (apart from starting and finishing at the same vertex) is called a Hamiltonian cycle.

Example 7.1 By listing all the different Hamiltonian cycles on the network below, find the length of the minimum tour.

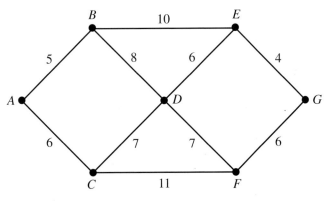

Step 1: Choose a starting vertex.

Start at vertex *A*.

Step 2: Find the Hamiltonian cycles, by inspection.

There are only two possible Hamiltonian cycles on this particular network.

ABEGFDCA
ABDEGFCA

Step 3: Calculate the weight of each cycle.

ABEGFDCA   has total length 45
ABDEGFCA   has total length 46

The minimum tour has length 45.

In practical problems there are usually some vertices that are not directly connected and sometimes an indirect route may be shorter than a direct route.

Note:
We can start at any vertex since a Hamiltonian cycle must pass through every vertex and the edges are not directed.

Note:
Once we have listed a cycle we do not need to list the same cycle in reverse.

Example 7.2 Construct a complete network of shortest routes for the network in Example 7.1.

Step 1: Find the shortest routes between pairs of vertices.

	A	B	C	D	E	F	G
A	–	5	6	13	15	17	19
B	5	–	11	8	10	15	14
C	6	11	–	7	13	11	17
D	13	8	7	–	6	7	10
E	15	10	13	6	–	10	4
F	17	15	11	7	10	–	6
G	19	14	17	10	4	6	–

Tip:
The shortest routes may be found by inspection, rather than formally using Dijkstra's algorithm.

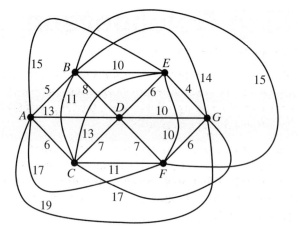

If we were asked to find the shortest Hamiltonian cycle on the
network in Example 7.2, we could not list them all.

Starting from *A* there are six choices for the second vertex, then five
for the third, four for the fourth, and so on. This gives $6! = 720$
cycles, but each cycle has been counted twice (once in each direction)
so there are 360 distinct cycles.

There is, at present, no algorithm for finding a solution to the
Travelling Salesperson problem; however, we can find limits within
which the solution must lie. We will mostly consider the classical
problem on a complete network of shortest distances.

SKILLS CHECK 7A: Practical problems and the classical problem

1 The network below shows the time, in hours, to travel by car between seven towns.

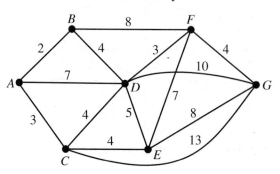

How long would it take to travel from *A* through *D, B, F, E, G, C* in that order and then return to *A*?
What does this tell you about the solution to the Travelling Salesperson problem on this network?

2 The distance matrix (distances in km) for a network is
$$\begin{array}{c} \\ A \\ B \\ C \\ D \end{array} \begin{array}{c} \begin{array}{cccc} A & B & C & D \end{array} \\ \left[\begin{array}{cccc} - & 4 & 3 & 8 \\ 4 & - & 2 & 3 \\ 3 & 2 & - & - \\ 8 & 3 & - & - \end{array} \right] \end{array}$$

a Show that the shortest distance from *A* to *D* is less than 8 km.

b Find the shortest distance from *C* to *D* and hence construct a distance matrix showing shortest
distances.

c Find the length of the cycle $A - B - C - D - A$, according to your matrix of shortest distances.

d Write down the edges that would be travelled in following the cycle from part **c**.

7.2 Nearest neighbour method

Determination of an upper bound by nearest neighbour method.

Since the Travelling Salesperson problem requires the shortest tour that passes through every vertex, the length of any tour that passes through every vertex must be an upper bound for the length of the solution to the Travelling Salesperson problem.

One way to find a tour that passes through every vertex exactly once is to use the nearest neighbour method. This method will not always work on a practical problem, but on a complete network of shortest distances it will always produce a tour through every vertex and it will often produce quite a short tour.

Start from any vertex.

- Choose the least-weight edge that joins this vertex to a vertex that has not already been visited. Add this edge to the cycle being formed, choose the vertex that has been joined to the cycle and repeat this step.

- If no edge can be chosen and all the vertices have been chosen add the edge that joins the current vertex back to the original vertex to complete the cycle.

Example 7.3 **a** Apply the nearest neighbour method to the network in Example 7.2 to find a tour starting from vertex A.

b Give the length of this tour.

Step 1: Find either the network or the table of edge weights.

	A	B	C	D	E	F	G
A	–	5	6	13	15	17	19
B	5	–	11	8	10	15	14
C	6	11	–	7	13	11	17
D	13	8	7	–	6	7	10
E	15	10	13	6	–	10	4
F	17	15	11	7	10	–	6
G	19	14	17	10	4	6	–

Step 2: Start at A and find the nearest vertex. Record the edge and its weight.

From A, the nearest neighbour is B. $\qquad AB = 5$

Step 3: From this vertex find the nearest vertex not yet visited. Record the edge and its weight.

From B, the nearest neighbour not yet visited is D. $\qquad BD = 8$

Step 4: Repeat step 3 until all vertices have been visited.

From D, the nearest neighbour not yet visited is E. $\qquad DE = 6$

From E, the nearest neighbour not yet visited is G. $\qquad EG = 4$

From G, the nearest neighbour not yet visited is F. $\qquad GF = 6$

From F, the nearest neighbour not yet visited is C. $\qquad FC = 11$

Note:
The method sometimes involves choosing quite long edges towards the end of the cycle.

Step 5: Close the tour by returning to the start.

From C, return to the start at A. $\qquad CA = 6$

Step 6: Add up the total length of the tour.

Total length of tour $= 5 + 8 + 6 + 4 + 6 + 11 + 6 = 46$.

The tour $A - B - D - E - G - F - C - A$ has length 46.

Note the similarity between the nearest neighbour method and Prim's algorithm. It is important that we do not confuse the two, with Prim we choose the least-weight edge from *all the vertices* that are in the tree, whereas in the nearest neighbour method we choose the least-weight edge from the *current vertex only*.

The solution to Example 7.3 gives an upper bound to the length of the solution of the Travelling Salesperson problem on the network. We may write:

$$\text{TSP} \leqslant 46$$

By using other vertices as the starting vertex we may get different upper bounds. Since each of these will be greater than or equal to TSP, the smallest (least upper bound) will be the closest to the unknown value TSP.

	A	B	C	D	E	F	G
A	–	5	6	13	15	17	19
B	5	–	11	8	10	15	14
C	6	11	–	7	13	11	17
D	13	8	7	–	6	7	10
E	15	10	13	6	–	10	4
F	17	15	11	7	10	–	6
G	19	14	17	10	4	6	–

Starting from B: $B-A-C-D-E-G-F-B = 49$
Starting from C: $C-A-B-D-E-G-F-C = 46$
Starting from D: $D-E-G-F-C-A-B-D = 46$
Starting from E: $E-G-F-D-C-A-B-E = 45$
Starting from F: $F-G-E-D-C-A-B-F = 49$
Starting from G: $G-E-D-C-A-B-F-G = 49$
        or $G-E-D-F-C-A-B-G = 53$

There are only really four different tours:

$$A-B-E-G-F-D-C-A = 45$$
$$A-B-D-E-G-F-C-A = 46$$
$$A-B-F-G-E-D-C-A = 49$$
$$A-B-G-E-D-F-C-A = 53$$

The least upper bound found by this method is 45, so $\text{TSP} \leqslant 45$.

SKILLS CHECK **7B: Nearest neighbour method**

1 The network below shows the time, in hours, to travel by car between seven towns.

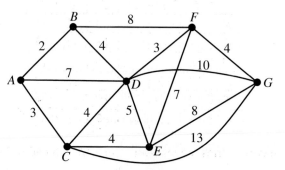

Use the nearest neighbour method to construct a tour starting from A.
What does this tell you about the solution to the Travelling Salesperson problem on this network?

2 a Apply the nearest neighbour method, starting from A, to the matrix on the right.

b Do you get a different tour by using a different starting point?

$$\begin{array}{c c c c c} & A & B & C & D \\ A & \begin{bmatrix} - & 4 & 3 & 7 \\ B & 4 & - & 2 & 3 \\ C & 3 & 2 & - & 5 \\ D & 7 & 3 & 5 & - \end{bmatrix} \end{array}$$

3 Apply the nearest neighbour method, starting from A, to the matrix on the right.

Describe what happens and explain why the method fails to find a tour.

$$\begin{array}{c c c c c} & A & B & C & D \\ A & \begin{bmatrix} - & 4 & 3 & - \\ B & 4 & - & 2 & 3 \\ C & 3 & 2 & - & 5 \\ D & - & 3 & 5 & - \end{bmatrix} \end{array}$$

4 The diagram shows a network of roads. The number on each edge is the length, in km, of the road. A salesman is to visit all the vertices before returning to the start vertex.

a State the number of different possible Hamiltonian cycles.

b Use the nearest neighbour algorithm starting from A to find an upper bound for the length of a minimum tour.

c By deleting A, find a lower bound for the length of a minimum tour.

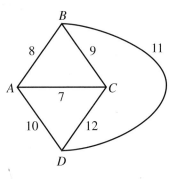

7.3 Finding a lower bound

Determination of a lower bound using a minimum spanning tree on a reduced network.

We now need to find a lower bound for the solution to the Travelling Salesperson problem. The following method gives such a lower bound for the classical problem, but it can give 'false' lower bounds for practical problems (i.e. give a value that is clearly bigger than the shortest solution).

- Delete one vertex and all the edges joined to it to form a reduced network.
- Construct a minimum spanning tree for this reduced network.
- Add the length of this minimum spanning tree to the weights of the two shortest edges that were removed.

Note:
To find a useful lower bound we need to calculate a length that is achievable as the length of the shortest tour through every vertex for some networks and never exceeds the length of the shortest tour on any network.

Example 7.4

Step 1: Delete the row and column for A. Construct a minimum spanning tree for the remaining matrix.

By deleting vertex A, find a lower bound for the length of the minimum tour through all the vertices on the network in Example 7.3. With A deleted, the minimum spanning tree has weight 31.

	B	C	D	E	F	G
B	–	11	8	10	15	14
C	11	–	7	13	11	17
D	(8)	7	–	6	7	10
E	10	13	(6)	–	10	4
F	15	11	7	10	–	(6)
G	14	17	10	(4)	6	–

$EG = 4$
$DE = 6$
$FG = 6$
$CD = 7$
$BD = \underline{8}$
31

Step 2: Find the two shortest edges from A.

The two shortest edges from A are $AB = 5$ and $AC = 6$.

Step 3: Add the weights from step 2 to the weight of the minimum spanning tree from step 1 to get a lower bound.

This gives the lower bound $31 + 11 = 42$.

Hence $42 \leqslant$ shortest tour $\leqslant 45$.

Note:
It is not usually necessary to show the working for constructing the minimum spanning tree.

Note:
This is a narrow range, and in practice we could just use common sense to check whether there is a tour that is shorter than 45.

By choosing a different vertex we may be able to get a larger lower bound; the greatest lower bound will be the one that is closest to TSP.

Deleting B gives $29 + 13 = 42$
Deleting C gives $29 + 13 = 42$
Deleting D gives $31 + 13 = 44$
Deleting E gives $31 + 10 = 41$
Deleting F gives $28 + 13 = 41$
Deleting G gives $31 + 10 = 41$

Hence,

$$44 \leqslant \text{TSP} \leqslant 45$$

Inspection shows that 44 is not the length of a tour through all the vertices.

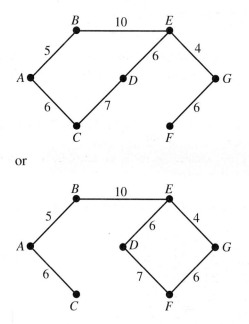

or

So the minimum tour through all the vertices must have length 45:

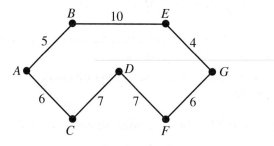

Note:
In this case we have not only given bounds for the length of the shortest tour but we have also found the minimum tour through all the vertices. In general it is difficult to solve the Travelling Salesperson problem and you are usually only required to find an upper bound, a lower bound, or both.

For this problem, the solution to the classical problem is also the solution to the practical problem, but this would not necessarily be the case since edges in the classical problem can involve passing through 'hidden' vertices in the practical problem. For example, $AD = 13$ is really $A - B - D = 5 + 8 = 13$.

1 The network below shows the time, in hours, to travel by car between seven towns.

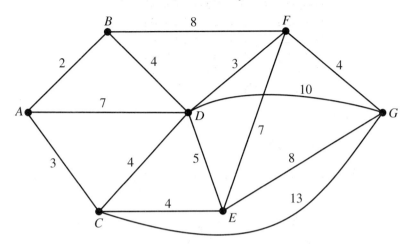

Find the minimum spanning tree for the network above with vertex D, and all the edges directly joined to D, deleted. Hence find a lower bound for the solution to the Travelling Salesperson problem on this network.

2 What can you deduce from your answers to question **1** of the Skills Checks 7A, 7B and 7C about the solution to the Travelling Salesperson problem for this network?
State the quickest journey time for a tour around the network, starting and ending at A and visiting every other vertex. Give the route for such a tour.

3 The table gives the distances in metres between points where footpaths meet.

	A	B	C	D	E	F
A	–	14	22	24	20	18
B	14	–	26	20	24	23
C	22	26	–	36	32	31
D	24	20	36	–	34	32
E	20	24	32	34	–	30
F	18	23	31	32	30	–

a Use the nearest neighbour method, starting from A, to obtain an upper bound for the minimum tour through these six meeting points.

b By initially ignoring vertex A, find a lower bound for the length of the minimum tour through the six meeting points.

4 a Find an upper bound for the Travelling Salesperson problem on the distance network below.

$$\begin{array}{c} & \begin{array}{cccc} A & B & C & D \end{array} \\ \begin{array}{c} A \\ B \\ C \\ D \end{array} & \left[\begin{array}{cccc} - & 4 & 3 & 7 \\ 4 & - & 2 & 3 \\ 3 & 2 & - & 5 \\ 7 & 3 & 5 & - \end{array} \right] \end{array}$$

b By initially ignoring vertex A, find a lower bound for the Travelling Salesperson problem on the same network.

c Using just your values from parts **a** and **b**, what can you deduce about the shortest cycle through all the vertices?

Questions **5**, **6** *and* **7** *refer to the following table, which shows the times, in minutes, to travel between four places.*

	A	B	C	D
A	–	13	12	15
B	13	–	14	16
C	12	14	–	17
D	15	16	17	–

5 a Starting from each of the vertices in turn, find four upper bounds for the length of the minimum travelling time to visit each of the vertices before returning to the start vertex.

   b State the best upper bound.

6 a By deleting each of the vertices, one at a time, find four lower bounds for the length of a minimum travelling time.

   b State the best lower bound.

7 a By using your answers to questions **5** and **6**, write down an interval of minimum width that contains the length of an optimal tour.

   b For a Travelling Salesperson problem, the upper bound is the same as the lower bound. State the conclusion that can be deduced.

   c For a Travelling Salesperson problem, the upper bound is lower than the lower bound. State the conclusion that can be deduced.

Examination practice   Travelling Salesperson problem

1 A company based in Rochdale produces a free newspaper for distribution locally. The table shows the six surrounding towns that receive the free paper. The figures represent the time, in minutes, to travel between the towns. The company delivery van has to travel from Rochdale to each one of the other towns, before returning to Rochdale.

	Rochdale	Castleton	Middleton	Shaw	Milnrow	Littleborough	Whitworth
Rochdale	–	3	7	8	6	5	4
Castleton	3	–	9	6	8	7.5	6.5
Middleton	7	9	–	14	12	11.5	12
Shaw	8	6	14	–	13	12	11
Milnrow	6	8	12	13	–	10	9
Littleborough	5	7.5	11.5	12	10	–	8
Whitworth	4	6.5	12	11	9	8	–

a Find a minimum connector for the seven towns, stating its length.

b Use the nearest neighbour algorithm, starting from Rochdale, to find an upper bound for a tour of the seven towns.

c By deleting Rochdale from the minimum connector found in part **a**, obtain a lower bound for a tour of the seven towns.

[AQA(A) Jan 2001]

2 Roger, a football supporter, is to visit each of six football grounds. He decides to travel from one ground to the next until he has visited all of the grounds, starting and finishing at Man. City. The following table shows the distances, in miles, between the grounds.

	Man. City	Burnley	Crewe	Preston	Stockport	Tranmere
Man. City	–	19	26	32	8	31
Burnley	19	–	43	21	22	36
Crewe	26	43	–	42	19	23
Preston	32	21	42	–	36	26
Stockport	8	22	19	36	–	27
Tranmere	31	36	23	26	27	–

a Use the nearest neighbour algorithm, starting and finishing at Man. City, to find an upper bound for the total distance Roger must travel.

b By initially ignoring Man. City, find a lower bound for the total distance he must travel in visiting the six grounds.

c Using your answers to parts **a** and **b**, write down inequalities for *D*, the total distance, in miles, that Roger has to travel. [AQA(A) Jan 2002]

3 A message is to be taken by a secretary to each of five classrooms. The secretary is based in the school office and will go to each classroom once before returning to the school office.

The table gives the times, in seconds, taken by the secretary to walk between pairs of rooms.

	Office	Room 1	Room 2	Room 3	Room 4	Room 5
Office	–	44	52	54	50	48
Room 1	44	–	56	50	54	53
Room 2	52	56	–	66	62	61
Room 3	54	50	66	–	64	62
Room 4	50	54	62	64	–	60
Room 5	48	53	61	62	60	–

a i The secretary leaves the office and visits rooms 1, 2, 3, 4 and 5 in that order before returning to the office.
Find the walking time for this tour.

ii Explain why this answer may be considered as an upper bound for the minimum total walking time for the secretary's tour.

b Use the nearest neighbour algorithm, starting from the office, to obtain an improved upper bound.

c By initially ignoring the office, find a lower bound for the walking time of the secretary's tour. [AQA(A) Nov 2003]

4 The distance matrix on the right represents a network of paths connecting five houses. The values represent the times, in minutes, to walk between the houses.

	A	B	C	D	E
A	–	8	4	7	3
B	8	–	10	15	10
C	4	10	–	9	6
D	7	15	9	–	9
E	3	10	6	9	–

Alan lives in house A. He wants to walk to each of the other houses and return to his own house in the minimum time possible.

a How long will it take Alan to walk the route $A - B - C - D - E - A$?

b Use the nearest neighbour algorithm to find a different tour through all the vertices, starting and ending at A. Calculate how long it will take Alan to walk this route.

c Use your answers to parts **a** and **b** to deduce an upper bound for Alan's minimum journey time.

d By initially ignoring vertex E, find a lower bound for Alan's minimum journey time.

5 The diagram on the right shows the tracks on a small railway network. The vertices represent stations and the distances are in miles. The route from A to C is a scenic route through a long and winding valley.

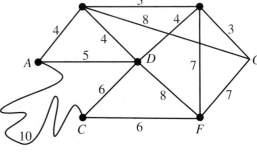

A station inspector wants to use the railway to visit each station starting and finishing at A, but as she does not enjoy train travel very much she wants to find the shortest possible tour.

a Use the nearest neighbour algorithm starting from A to find an upper bound for the length of the minimum tour.

b Explain why the nearest neighbour algorithm can sometimes fail to find a tour.

c By initially ignoring vertex D, find a lower bound for the shortest tour.

d Find a tour for which the length is greater than the lower bound from part **b** but less than the upper bound from part **a**.

6 The distance matrix on the right represents a network of paths connecting six inns. The values represent the distances between the inns, in units of 100 metres.

	A	B	C	D	E	F
A	–	3	2	7	8	18
B	3	–	4	5	6	10
C	2	4	–	3	9	12
D	7	5	3	–	8	9
E	8	6	9	8	–	8
F	18	10	12	9	8	–

A charity event requires contestants to walk to each of the six inns, starting and finishing at A.

a Use the nearest neighbour algorithm to find an upper bound for the distance that the contestants must walk.

b By initially ignoring vertex F, find a lower bound for the distance that the contestants must walk.

8 Linear programming

8.1 Formulating linear programming problems

When formulating a linear programming problem:

- identify the control variables
- identify the objective as a function of the variables
- identify the constraints as functions of the variables.

Control variables are the quantities for which there is some degree of control. The problem is to determine the values that these variables should take. For simple problems there are typically no more than three control variables.

The **objective** is either to maximise or to minimise the objective function. The objective function is a linear function of the control variables and usually represents either a cost or a profit.

The values of the control variables are limited by **constraints**. These are linear inequalities that model the physical restrictions on the values of the variables. Sometimes there is an additional requirement that one or more of the variables take integer values.

Linear programming problems have a linear objective function and linear constraints. This means that if the variables are x, y and z then the objective is of the form

$$ax + by + cz$$

and the constraints are of the form

$$dx + ey + fz \geqslant \text{constant} \quad \text{or} \quad dx + ey + fz \leqslant \text{constant}$$
for constants a, b, c, d, e, f

Example 8.1 A manufacturer makes three types of health drinks: Xtralight, Yog and Zingo. The manufacturing process of each drink involves two stages: production and packing. The table below shows the time that one litre of each type of drink takes at each stage.

	Production time	**Packing time**
Xtralight	20 minutes	10 minutes
Yog	30 minutes	8 minutes
Zingo	15 minutes	12 minutes

The production stage takes place during the mornings. Only one type of drink can be in the production stage at any one time, and the total time spent in production must not exceed 4 hours each day.

The packing stage takes place during the afternoons. Only one type of drink can be in the packing stage at any one time, and the total time spent in packing must not exceed 2 hours each day.

The manufacturer makes a profit of £1.60 for each litre of Xtralight manufactured, £2.50 for each litre of Yog and £1.80 for each litre of Zingo.

The manufacturer wants to determine the amounts of each of the three drinks that should be manufactured to maximise the profit. Assume that the manufacturer can sell all the drink that is manufactured, whether complete litres or not.

a Identify the control variables for this problem.

b Write down the objective function for the problem.

c Write down all the constraints on the control variables.

Step 1: Decide which values can be changed and identify the units in which they are measured.

a Let x be the amount of Xtralight manufactured each day (in litres),
y be the amount of Yog manufactured each day (in litres),
z be the amount of Zingo manufactured each day (in litres).

> **Note:**
> The variables will usually either be 'number of …' or 'amount or …'.

Step 2: Identify the quantity to be maximised or minimised.

b Maximise $160x + 250y + 180z$.

> **Note:**
> The objective should include 'maximise' or 'minimise'. Sometimes the objective function is given a name, such as: maximise $P = …$

Step 3: Work through the information given to find every restriction on the values of the variables. Express these as linear inequalities.

c Constraints:

$$20x + 30y + 15z \leqslant 240 \quad \text{(production time)}$$
$$10x + 8y + 12z \leqslant 120 \quad \text{(packing time)}$$
$$\text{and} \quad x \geqslant 0, y \geqslant 0, z \geqslant 0 \quad \text{(non-negativity constraints)}$$

Step 4: Use scaling to simplify the coefficients in the constraints.

$$4x + 6y + 3z \leqslant 48$$
$$5x + 4y + 6z \leqslant 60$$
$$x \geqslant 0, y \geqslant 0, z \geqslant 0$$

The information may be presented in a less straightforward way.

Example 8.2 Consider the problem in Example 8.1. Represent each of the situations below as a linear constraint. The situations happen independently of each other, not all at the same time.

a The amount of Zingo manufactured must not exceed twice the amount of Xtralight manufactured.

b The amount of Xtralight manufactured must be less than the total amount of Yog and Zingo.

c For each litre of Xtralight manufactured at least two litres of Zingo must be manufactured.

> **Note:**
> Be careful about words like 'not exceed', 'less than', 'at least'.

Step 1: Express each constraint as a linear inequality in the variables.

a $z \leqslant 2x$

b $x < y + z$

c $z \geqslant 2x$

> **Note:**
> Check some critical values for each constraint:
> **a** $x = 10, z = 20$
> **b** $x = 10, y = 8, z = 2$
> **c** $x = 10, z = 20$

Sometimes we are given additional information that enables us to eliminate one of the variables from a three variable problem and reduce it to a two variable problem.

Example 8.3 Consider the problem in Example 8.1, together with all three constraints from Example 8.2. Eliminate the z-variable and hence reduce the problem to a two-variable linear programming problem.

Step 1: Write z in terms of the other variables.

From the first and third constraints in Example 8.2 we have $z = 2x$.

Maximise $520x + 250y$

Subject to the constraints:

$$50x + 30y \leqslant 240 \quad \Rightarrow \quad 5x + 3y \leqslant 24$$
$$34x + 8y \leqslant 120 \quad \Rightarrow \quad 17x + 4y \leqslant 60$$
$$x < y + 2x \quad \Rightarrow \quad x + y > 0$$
$$\text{and} \quad x \geqslant 0, y \geqslant 0$$

SKILLS CHECK 8A: Formulating linear programming problems

1 Three friends are making fruit cocktails using apple juice, banana juice and clementine juice.
Let a be the amount of apple juice used, in ml; b be the amount of banana juice used, in ml;
and c be the amount of clementine juice used, in ml. The amount in the cocktail is $a + b + c$ ml.

Diane wants to have equal amounts of banana juice and clementine juice in her cocktail and she also
wants less apple juice than banana juice.

   a Write down constraints using a, b and c for Diane's cocktail.

Edward wants to have no banana juice and he wants more than twice as much apple juice as
clementine juice.

   b Write down constraints using a, b and c for Edward's cocktail.

Fiona wants no more than a quarter of her cocktail to be apple juice.

   c Write down constraints using a, b and c for Fiona's cocktail.

2 Auntie makes cards which she sells on her market stall. She is currently working on two designs:
Xmas and Yachts. Each Xmas card takes her 20 minutes to make and uses two pieces of card and
some glitter, each Yachts card takes her 30 minutes to make and uses one piece of card and some
string.

Auntie has plenty of glitter and string but she only has 10 pieces of card left. She does not want to
spend more than 3 hours making the cards. She will be able to sell all the cards she makes, and she
makes a profit of 25 pence on every card. Auntie wants to make as big a profit as possible.

   a Define appropriate variables for Auntie's problem.

   b Write down an inequality, in terms of your variables, to represent the constraint on the number of
pieces of card available.

   c Write down an inequality to represent the constraint on Auntie's time.

   d Write down two further inequalities that represent constraints on the variables.

   e Write down an expression to be maximised in Auntie's problem.

3 Holly and Robin have set up a small business making hand-made greetings cards.
Holly cuts the cards to size and writes the words inside the cards, Robin then decorates the front of
each card with an appropriate design.

They make two types of card, 'snow scene' and 'trees'. Holly can cut and write 16 'snow scene' cards
or 9 'trees' cards each hour. Robin can decorate 10 'snow scene' cards or 15 'trees' cards each hour.

Holly works for 4 hours on Monday and 3 hours on Tuesday. Robin works for 1 hour on Wednesday
and 2 hours on Thursday. On Friday they both pack the cards they have made and take them to a
shop to be sold.

The shop pay Holly and Robin £2 for each 'snow scene' card and £1.80 for each 'trees' card, the
'snow scene' cards cost 90p each to make and the 'trees' cards cost 75p each to make. Holly and
Robin want to maximise their profit.

Let s be the number of 'snow scene' cards that they make each week and t be the number of 'trees' cards that they make each week.

a Write down and simplify an inequality to represent the constraint on the number of cards that Holly can process in a week.

b Write down and simplify an inequality to represent the constraint on the number of cards that Robin can process in a week.

c Write down and simplify an expression for the profit to be maximised.

Graphical solution of two-variable problems.

Two-variable linear programming problems can be solved graphically. Plot lines representing the equality case for each constraint and then shade the region where the inequality is *not* satisfied. The region that is never shaded is the **feasible region** where all the constraints are satisfied.

Next find the point of the feasible region where the objective takes its optimum value.

To plot a constraint, first plot the equation representing its limiting case. To plot a line use the coordinates of two points on the line and then join them. Usually these will be the points where the line crosses the axes.

> **Note:**
> We do not usually worry about whether or not the edges of the feasible region are included at this stage.

Example 8.4 Find the coordinates where the line $5x + 3y = 24$ crosses the axes.

Step 1: Find the value of x when $y = 0$ and the value of y when $x = 0$.

$5x = 24 \Rightarrow x = 4.8$ (4.8, 0)
$3y = 24 \Rightarrow y = 8$ (0, 8)

In the exam, the axes are usually pre-printed on an insert sheet. If the axes cannot accommodate the points where a line crosses the axes, calculate another point on the line.

> **Note:**
> Just 'cover up' the y-term to set $y = 0$ and then do the same for x.

Example 8.5 Calculate the coordinates of the point on the line $5x + 3y = 24$ at which $x = 3$.

Step 1: Set $x = 3$ to find y. When $x = 3$ we have $15 + 3y = 24 \Rightarrow 3y = 9 \Rightarrow y = 3$ (3, 3)

Shade the side of the line where the inequality is *not* satisfied. To find out which side this is choose any point that is not on the line and check whether or not the inequality holds. Often it is convenient to use the origin as our test point (unless this lies on the line).

For example, the point (0, 0) clearly does satisfy the inequality $5x + 3y \leqslant 24$ so the side of the line that does not include (0, 0) would be shaded.

The graph on the right shows the constraint $5x + 3y \leqslant 24$ with the region where the inequality is not satisfied shaded.

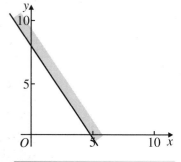

> **Note:**
> You do not need to shade out the whole of the region above the line; this is implied.

Example 8.6 Represent all the constraints from Example 8.3 on a single graph, shading the regions where the inequalities are not satisfied.

Step 1: For each inequality, plot the points where it crosses the axes and join these with a straight line. Then test a point not on the line to determine which side of the line the inequality is not satisfied, and shade this side.

$$5x + 3y \leqslant 24 \qquad (4.8, 0), (0, 8)$$
$$17x + 4y \leqslant 60 \qquad (3\tfrac{9}{17}, 0), (0, 15), (2, 6.5)$$
$$x + y > 0 \qquad (0, 0), (5, -5)$$
$$x \geqslant 0$$
$$y \geqslant 0$$

Having identified the feasible region, find the point within the feasible region where the objective is optimised (in this case where $520x + 250y$ is a maximum).

Having identified the feasible region, find the point within the feasible region where the objective is optimised (in this case where $520x + 250y$ is a maximum).

The strategy is to plot a line for which the objective takes some fixed value and then identify the direction in which this line would move when the value of the objective increases. Then identify the point of the feasible region where the objective takes its greatest (or least) value.

Note:
The constraint $x + y > 0$ is redundant (except to exclude the origin from the feasible region).

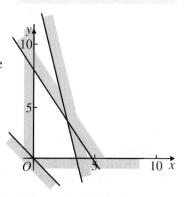

Note:
If there is a simple common multiple of the coefficients it is a good idea to use this as the fixed value; there is no such value here.

Example 8.7 Plot the line $520x + 250y = 1000$ on the graph from Example 8.6.

Step 1: Find where the line cuts the axes.

Step 2: Plot the line by joining these points.

The line passes through $(1\tfrac{12}{13}, 0)$ and $(0, 4)$.

The line of constant profit that we have drawn has $520x + 250y = 1000$.

For different values of the profit we get a set of parallel lines.

To find the direction of increasing profit, calculate the value of the profit at a point not on the line already drawn. For example, at $(0, 0)$ the value of $520x + 250y$ is 0, so the direction of increasing profit is perpendicular to the plotted line, pointing away from the origin.

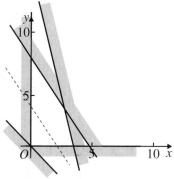

Show this with arrows indicating the direction in which the line should be moved to achieve the maximum or minimum feasible value, depending on whether the problem wants a maximum or a minimum value of the objective function.

The maximum feasible value occurs at the vertex where $5x + 3y = 24$ meets $17x + 4y = 60$. Using simultaneous equations (or a solver on a graphical calculator) this point is where $x = 2\tfrac{22}{31}$ and $y = 3\tfrac{15}{31}$ or approximately $(2.71, 3.48)$ with an associated profit of 2280 exactly.

An alternative way to find the solution is to calculate the coordinates of each vertex of the feasible region and then evaluate the profit at each vertex.

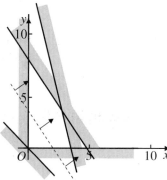

The graphical method has given us the solution that each day the manufacturer should produce $2\tfrac{22}{31}$ litres of Xtralight, $3\tfrac{15}{31}$ litres of Yog and $5\tfrac{13}{31}$ litres of Zingo to give a profit of £22.80 each day.

If the manufacturer decided that only full litres of the drinks could be sold this would be an **integer programming** problem. The strategies for solving integer programming problems are beyond the scope of the examination. All that is required is to check integer points to find the best feasible point where the variables take integer values, using the same graph as earlier.

Note:
$z = 2x$.

Using the constraint $5x + 3y \leq 24$:

> if $x = 2$, the maximum feasible integer value of y is 4, giving a
>   profit of 2040
> if $x = 1$, $y = 6$, giving a profit of 2020
> if $x = 0$, $y = 8$, giving a profit of 2000

Using the constraint $17x + 4y \leq 60$:

> if $x = 3$, $y = 2$, giving a profit of 2060
> x cannot equal 4

So the solution to the integer programming problem is

> $x = 3$, $y = 2$, $z = 6$ and a daily profit of £20.60

SKILLS CHECK **8B: Solving two-variable linear programming problems graphically**

1 The graph on the right shows the feasible region of a linear programming problem.

The vertices of the feasible region are $(0, 0)$, $(80, 0)$, $(30, 50)$, $(20, 50)$ and $(0, 30)$.

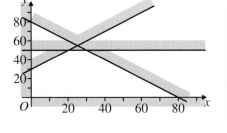

a Calculate the maximum value of $x + 2y$ on this feasible region.

b Find the five inequalities that define the feasible region.

2 Consider the following linear programming problem:

Maximise	$P = 3x + 2y$
subject to	$5x + y \leq 100$
	$4x - 3y \geq 12$
	$x + 2y \geq 10$
and	$x \geq 0, y \geq 0.$

a Represent the feasible region graphically.

b Calculate the coordinates of the vertices of the feasible region and hence find the values of x and y at which P is a maximum.

3 This question is based on the situation that you modelled in Skills check 8A, question **2**.
Use your results from that question as a basis for the answer to this question.
Auntie makes cards which she sells on her market stall. She is currently working on two designs: Xmas and Yachts. Each Xmas card takes her 20 minutes to make and uses two pieces of card and some glitter, each Yachts card takes her 30 minutes to make and uses one piece of card and some string.

Auntie has plenty of glitter and string but she only has 10 pieces of card left. She does not want to spend more than 3 hours making the cards. She will be able to sell all the cards she makes, and she makes a profit of 25 pence on every card. Auntie wants to make as big a profit as possible.

a Draw a graph to show the feasible region for Auntie's problem.

b Show the direction of the objective line on your graph.

c Use your graph to solve Auntie's problem.

4 a Represent the feasible region of the following linear programming problem graphically.

$$\text{Maximise} \qquad P = 109x + 105y$$

$$\text{subject to} \qquad 27x + 64y \leqslant 1008$$
$$3x + 2y \leqslant 90$$
$$\text{and} \qquad x \geqslant 0, y \geqslant 0.$$

b Calculate the values of x and y that maximise P.

c Suppose that the values of x and y must be integers. By checking points near the solution previously found, find the integer feasible values of x and y that maximise P and the maximum value of P in this case.

5 Solve the following linear programming problem, using a graphical method.

a Maximise $2x + y$ subject to

$$x \geqslant 10, \quad y \geqslant 10, \quad y \leqslant x \quad \text{and} \quad x + y \leqslant 50.$$

b i Maximise $2x + 2y$ subject to the same constraints.

ii Find the number of different combinations that correspond to this maximum.

6 Each day during April a gardener plants two different types of onion sets: English and Spanish.

Each day she must plant at least 20 sets in total.
English onion sets need to be prepared for 2 minutes before planting, whereas Spanish sets only need 1 minute of preparation time.
English sets need 0.5 litres of plant food, but Spanish sets need 1 litre of plant food.
Each day there are 90 minutes available for preparing the sets for planting and there are 45 litres of plant food available.

Each day the gardener plants x English onion sets and y Spanish onion sets.
The gardener wishes to plant as many onion sets as possible.

a Formulate the gardener's situation as a linear programming problem.

b Draw a suitable diagram to enable the problem to be solved graphically, indicating the feasible region and the direction of the objective line.

c Find the maximum number of onion sets that can be planted each day.

7 A company uses a machine to produce two types of paper: cream and white.
Every hour the company must produce at least 20 reams of paper.
It takes 1.5 minutes to produce a ream of cream paper and 1 minute to produce a ream of white paper.
For every ream of cream paper it produces, the company must not produce more than double that number of reams of white paper.
Every hour the company produces x reams of cream paper and y reams of white paper.
The company makes a profit of 20p on each ream of cream paper and 30p on each ream of white paper.
The company wishes to find its minimum and maximum hourly profit.

a Formulate the company's situation as a linear programming problem.

b Draw a suitable diagram to enable the problem to be solved graphically, indicating the feasible region and the direction of the objective line.

c Find the minimum and maximum hourly profit for the company.

8 Each day a company makes and packs three different types of chair: standard, luxury and executive.
Each standard chair takes 30 minutes to make and 4 minutes to pack.
Each luxury chair takes 40 minutes to make and 4 minutes to pack.
Each executive chair takes 50 minutes to make and 5 minutes to pack.

Each day:

there are three workers available, each for eight hours a day, to make the chairs;
there is only one worker available for two hours to pack the chairs;
the company must make, and pack, at least 60% of the chairs as standard chairs;
the company must make, and pack, at least twice as many luxury chairs as executive chairs;
the company must make and pack at least 15 chairs.

Each day the company makes, and packs, x standard, y luxury and z executive chairs.
The company makes a profit of £3 on each standard chair, £5 on each luxury chair and £10 on each executive chair.
The company wishes to maximise its profit.
Formulate the company's situation as a linear programming problem.

Examination practice Linear programming

1 Stephanie works at a garden centre. Each day during May she has to make hanging baskets using three types of plant: ivy (I), lobelia (L) and primula (P).

She makes three different types of hanging basket: standard, superior and luxury.

Standard baskets contain 1 ivy, 2 lobelia and 3 primula plants.
Superior baskets contain 2 ivy, 3 lobelia and 3 primula plants.
Luxury baskets contain 3 ivy, 5 lobelia and 4 primula plants.

Each day Stephanie must use **at least** 30 ivy, 50 lobelia and 40 primula plants,
but **not** more than 200 plants in total; and **at least** 40% of the plants she uses must be lobelia.

In a day Stephanie makes x standard baskets, y superior baskets and z luxury baskets.
Find **five** inequalities in x, y and z which must be satisfied, simplifying each
inequality where possible.   [AQA(A) Nov 2002]

2 The Tony television company makes analogue and digital televisions. Both types of television require a number of component A and component B.

Each analogue television requires 2 of component A and 3 of component B.
Each digital television requires 4 of component A and 1 of component B.

Each day:

the company has 50 of component A and 24 of component B available; and
the company is to make at least 2 of each type of television, but no more than 20 in total.

The company sells each analogue television at a profit of £20 and each digital television at a profit of £25.
Each day, the company makes and sells x analogue and y digital televisions.
The company needs to find its minimum and maximum daily income, £T.

a Formulate the company's situation as a linear programming problem.

b Draw a suitable diagram to enable the problem to be solved graphically, indicating the feasible region and the direction of the objective line.

c Use your diagram to find the company's minimum and maximum daily income, £T.   [AQA(A) May 2002]

3 A company produces two types of gift box, standard and luxury.

Each day, the company produces x standard and y luxury gift boxes.
Each day, the company must produce at least 20 of each type and at least 70 in total.

The boxes are produced using three different machines.

Machine A must be used for at least 100 minutes each day.
Machine B is available for a maximum of 5 hours each day.
Machine C is available for a maximum of 8 hours each day.

The time taken to produce a standard box is:

2 minutes on machine A;
3 minutes on machine B; and
4 minutes on machine C.

A luxury box requires:

1 minute on machine A;
2 minutes on machine B; and
4 minutes on machine C.

The company wishes to produce the maximum number of boxes each day.

a Formulate the company's situation as a linear programming problem.

b Draw a suitable diagram to enable the problem to be solved graphically, indicating the feasible region.

c **i** Find the maximum number of boxes the company can produce each day.
ii Find the number of different combinations of standard and luxury boxes that would enable the company to produce this maximum total. [AQA(A) Jan 2003]

4 Tara is buying cakes for her work mates. She wants to buy at least ten cakes and spend as little as possible.

Cream cakes cost 60p each; doughnuts cost £1 for four, but cannot be bought individually; and éclairs cost £1.20 for three, but cannot be bought individually.

Tara decides to buy c cream cakes, d doughnuts and e éclairs, where c, d and e are integers with d a multiple of 4 and e a multiple of 3.

a Explain why Tara needs to minimise $60c + 25d + 40e$.

b Explain why the values are subject to the constraint $c + d + e \geqslant 10$.

c Find the cost of Tara's cheapest option when $d = 8$.

d Show that this is not the cheapest way for Tara to satisfy the constraints.

5 **a** Draw a graph to show the feasible region of the linear programming problem

Maximise $\quad x + 2y$

Subject to $\quad x + y \leqslant 4$
$\qquad\qquad\quad x \geqslant 1$
$\qquad\qquad\quad 2x + y \leqslant 6$
and $\qquad\quad x \geqslant 0, y \geqslant 0$

b Find the values of x and y that solve the problem.

6 George wants to buy some vegetables for a stew. Carrots cost 4p each and turnips cost 15p each.

George buys x carrots and y turnips.

a How much does it cost to buy x carrots and y turnips?

George does not want to spend more than 90p.

b Express this constraint as an inequality involving x and y.

George wants at least 5 carrots for each turnip in the stew.

c Express this constraint as an inequality involving x and y.

d Draw a graph to show the feasible region for this problem.

The amount of stew made is given by the rule $20 + x + 0.8y$.
George wants to make as much stew as possible.

e Use your graph to solve the problem.

Practice exam paper

Answer **all** questions.

Time allowed: 1 hour 30 minutes

A calculator **may** be used in this paper.

1 a Use a shuttle sort algorithm to rearrange the following numbers into ascending order, showing the new arrangement after each pass.

24, 16, 38, 49, 10, 15, 52, 28   *(4 marks)*

b State the number of comparisons and swaps on the first pass.   *(1 mark)*

c The original set of numbers is to be rearranged into ascending order using a bubble sort algorithm. State the number of comparisons and swaps on the first pass, using this algorithm.   *(2 marks)*

2 a Draw a bipartite graph representing the following adjacency matrix.

	1	2	3	4	5
A	1	0	0	0	1
B	0	1	1	1	0
C	1	0	0	0	1
D	0	1	1	1	0
E	1	0	0	0	1

(2 marks)

b If A, B, C, D, E represent five people and 1, 2, 3, 4, 5 represent five tasks to which they are to be assigned, explain why a complete matching is impossible.   *(1 mark)*

c Given that now C can be matched to 3, list all the different possible complete matchings of people to tasks.   *(2 marks)*

3 The following network has 10 vertices. The numbers represent the weight of each arc.

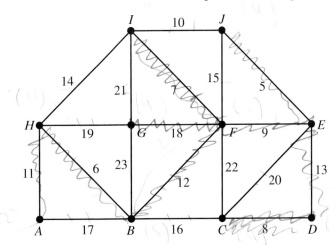

a Use Kruskal's algorithm, showing the order in which you select the edges, to find the minimum spanning tree for the network.   *(4 marks)*

b State the weight of your minimum spanning tree.   *(1 mark)*

c Draw your minimum spanning tree.   *(2 marks)*

d If Prim's algorithm, starting from A, had been used to find the minimum spanning tree, state which edge would have been the final edge to be chosen.   *(1 mark)*

e Find the length of an optimal Chinese Postman route around the network, starting and finishing at A.   *(3 marks)*

4 A student is using the algorithm below.

LINE 10   INPUT A, B
LINE 20   LET $C = A - 2 \times B$
LINE 30   LET $D = A + 2 \times B$
LINE 40   LET $E = 3 \times A \times A + C \times D$
LINE 50   LET $F = 4 \times (A - B)$
LINE 60   LET $G = \dfrac{E}{F}$
LINE 70   END

a Trace the algorithm in the case where $A = 7$ and $B = 3$. *(3 marks)*

b Write down the value of G in the case where $A = 20$ and $B = 13$. *(1 mark)*

5 a Draw the graph K_5. *(2 marks)*

b For the graph K_n, state, in terms of n,

i the total number of edges,

ii the number of edges in a minimum spanning tree,

iii the number of edges in a Hamiltonian cycle,

iv the condition for K_n to be Eulerian,

v the number of different Hamiltonian cycles. *(5 marks)*

c For the graph K_n, the length of an Eulerian cycle is the same as the length of a Hamiltonian cycle. State the value of n. *(1 mark)*

6 The diagram shows a network of roads connecting 12 towns. The number on each arc represents the travelling time, in minutes, between two towns.

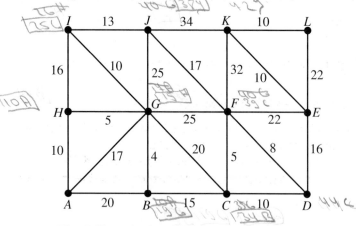

a Use Dijkstra's algorithm to find the shortest travelling time from A to L. State the corresponding route. *(6 marks)*

b Find the shortest travelling time from I to L. *(1 mark)*

c A road is to be built connecting towns I and L. The time taken to travel along this road will be x minutes. The new road will reduce the travelling time from I to L but not reduce the travelling time from A to L. Find the range of possible values of x. *(3 marks)*

7 Sarah is going to buy a house in one of five towns A, B, C, D or E.
Sarah is going to visit the five towns. She intends to travel from one town to the next until she has visited all of the towns before returning to her starting town.
The distances, in miles, between the towns are shown in the following table.

	A	B	C	D	E
A	–	21	20	23	18
B	21	–	23	21	19
C	20	23	–	15	14
D	23	21	15	–	16
E	18	19	14	16	–

a **i** Find the length of the tour *ADCEBA*. *(1 mark)*

    ii Find the length of the tour using the nearest neighbour algorithm starting from *A*. *(4 marks)*

b **i** By deleting *A*, find a lower bound for the length of a minimum tour. *(5 marks)*

    ii By deleting *D*, find another lower bound for the length of a minimum tour. *(3 marks)*

c Given that the length of a minimum tour is *T* kilometres, use your answers to parts **a** and **b** to write down the smallest interval within which *T* must lie. *(2 marks)*

8 Each day Stella is to make two types of loaves of bread: standard and luxury.
Each day she must make at least 40 standard loaves and at least 60 luxury loaves, but she can only make at most 200 loaves.
Each standard loaf costs 10p to make and takes 2 minutes in the oven, each luxury loaf costs 6p to make and takes 3 minutes in the oven.
Each day she has £15 to spend and the oven must be used for at least 5 hours.
She must make at least 50% more luxury than standard loaves, but not more than double the number of luxury to standard loaves.
Each day Stella makes *x* standard loaves and *y* luxury loaves.

a Show that Stella's situation can be modelled by the following inequalities:

$$x \geq 40, \quad y \geq 60, \quad x + y \leq 200, \quad 2x + 3y \geq 300, \quad 5x + 3y \leq 750,$$
$$y \leq 2x \quad \text{and} \quad 2y \geq 3x.$$

(4 marks)

b Draw a suitable diagram to enable the problem to be solved graphically, indicating the feasible region. *(7 marks)*

c State which inequality does not affect the feasible region. *(1 mark)*

d Each day Stella sells each loaf that she makes. Each standard loaf is sold for a profit of 40p and each luxury loaf for a profit of 50p.
By using an objective line, or otherwise, find Stella's maximum daily profit and the number of standard and luxury loaves corresponding to this maximum. *(3 marks)*

Answers

SKILLS CHECK 1A (page 2)

1

LINE	A	B	C	Comments
10	10			
20		5		
30			25	
40				$|C - A| = 15$ which is bigger than 0.1
50		3.5		
60				
30			12.25	
40				$|C - A| = 2.25$ which is bigger than 0.1
50		3.179		
60				
30			10.103	
40				$|C - A| = 0.103$ which is bigger than 0.1
50		3.162		
60				
30			10.000	
40				$|C - A| = 0.000264$ which is smaller than 0.1
70				**Display 3.16231942215**
80				

2

LINE	N	D	P	Comments
10	60			
20			2	
30		30		
40				$60 \neq 1$
50				$60 = 2 \times 30$ **display 2**
60	30			
30		15		
40				$30 \neq 1$
50				$30 = 2 \times 15$ **display 2**
60	15			
30		7		
40				$15 \neq 1$
50				$15 \neq 2 \times 7$
80			3	
90		5		
100				$15 \neq 1$
110				$15 = 3 \times 5$ **display 3**
120	5			
90		1		
100				$5 \neq 1$
110				$5 \neq 3 \times 1$
140			5	
90		1		
100				$5 \neq 1$
110				$5 = 5 \times 1$ **display 5**
120	1			
90		0		
100				$N = 1$ STOP

3 **a** This line checks whether we have found all the factors of N, with N being a power of 2.

b This line checks whether we have taken out all the factors that are powers of 2.

c These lines check whether 2 is a factor of N.

d These lines set up the algorithm for checking whether 2 is a repeated factor of N.

4

LINE	N	C	List	Sublist
10	8		28 64 37 59 21 54 47 33	
20	4	1		
30				28 21
40			21 64 37 59 28 54 47 33	21 28
50		2		
30				64 54
40			21 54 37 59 28 64 47 33	54 64
50		3		
30				37 47
40			21 54 37 59 28 64 47 33	37 47
50		4		
30				59 33
40			21 54 37 33 28 64 47 59	33 59
50		5		
60				
20	2	1		
30				21 37 28 47
40			21 54 28 33 37 64 47 59	21 28 37 47
50		2		
30				54 33 64 59
40			21 33 28 54 37 59 47 64	33 54 59 64
50		3		
60				
20	1	1		
30				21 33 28 54 37 59 47 64
40			21 28 33 37 47 54 59 64	21 28 33 37 47 54 59 64
50		2		
60			21 28 33 37 47 54 59 64	

5

N	C	Printed list
17	0	17
52	1	52
26	2	26
13	3	13
40	4	40
20	5	20
10	6	10
5	7	5
16	8	16
8	9	8
4	10	4
2	11	2
1	12	1 Output 12

6 $N = 5$, $A = 50$, $B = 522$, $S = 22$, $M = 10$, $D = 2.345$
Display: 10, 2.345

7 3, 5, 7, 9, 11   Sum equals 35

8 **a**

A	B	Printed list
1		1
	1	1
2		2
3		3
4		4
5		5
6		6
7		7
8		8
9		9

b We need to use a counter. For example, add the following lines:

LINE 25	Let $C = 2$
LINE 45	Increase C by 1
LINE 48	If $C = 10$, STOP

c There are various ways to do this, for example:

LINE 50	Replace B by $A + B$
LINE 60	Print the value of B
LINE 65	Increase C by 1
LINE 68	If $C = 10$, STOP
LINE 70	Go back to LINE 30

Or

LINE 30	Let D have the value $A + B$
LINE 40	Print the value of D
LINE 50	Replace A by B
LINE 60	Replace B by D
LINE 70	Go back to LINE 30

SKILLS CHECK 1B (page 8)

1 Initial list: 4 5 3 1 2

First pass:
4 5 3 1 2
4 3 5 1 2
4 3 1 5 2
4 3 1 2 5

Second pass:
3 4 1 2 5
3 1 4 2 5
3 1 2 4 5

Third pass:
1 3 2 4 5
1 2 3 4 5

Fourth pass: 1 2 3 4 5

Final list: 1 2 3 4 5

2 Initial list: 4   7 6 4 2 5
After first pass: 4 7   6 4 2 5
After second pass: 4 6 7   4 2 5
After third pass: 4 4 6 7   2 5
After fourth pass: 2 4 4 6 7   5
After fifth pass: 2 4 4 5 6 7

3 Initial list: 6 3 5 7 4 8 1 2 9

First pass: 3 5 4 1 2 6 7 8 9

Second pass: 1 2 3 5 4 6 7 8 9

Third pass: 1 2 3 4 5 6 7 8 9   List is sorted

4 a Original list: 31   17 25 13 21 34
After first pass: 31 17   25 13 21 34   swaps = 0
After second pass: 31 25 17   13 21 34   swaps = 1
After third pass: 31 25 17 13   21 34   swaps = 0
After fourth pass: 31 25 21 17 13   34   swaps = 2
After fifth pass: 34 31 25 21 17 13   swaps = 5

b Total swaps = 8
For a list of six numbers the maximum is $1 + 2 + 3 + 4 + 5 = 15$ swaps.

5 a 8, 7, 6, 5, 4, 3, 2, 1 $8 \div 2 = 4$

8   4
  7   3
   6   2
    5   1
4   8
  3   7
   2   6
    1   5

4, 3, 2, 1, 8, 7, 6, 5 $4 \div 2 = 2$
4   2   8   6
  3   1   7   5
2   4   6   8
  1   3   5   7

2, 1, 4, 3, 6, 5, 8, 7 $2 \div 2 = 1$

2 1 4 3 6 5 8 7
1 2 3 4 5 6 7 8
1, 2, 3, 4, 5, 6, 7, 8

b Sorting each sublist in the first pass requires 1 comparison and 1 swap, giving a total of 4 comparisons and 4 swaps in this pass.

Sorting each sublist in the second pass requires 4 comparisons and 2 swaps, giving a total of 8 comparisons and 4 swaps in this pass.

Sorting the list in the third pass requires 10 comparisons and 4 swaps.

This gives a total of 22 comparisons and 12 swaps.

c Using bubble sort would need $7 + 6 + 5 + 4 + 3 + 2 + 1 = 28$ comparisons.
So shell sort is more efficient.

6   4 3 7 2 7 1 8

First pass   3 2 1 4 7 7 8

Second pass   2 1 3 4 7 7 8

Third pass   1 2 3 4 7 7 8

Final list   1 2 3 4 7 7 8

7 First pass   3 5 8 3 2 4 8 3 2 $N = 4$
3   2   2
   5   4
     8   8
      3   3

New list   2 4 8 3 2 5 8 3 3
Second pass   2 4 8 3 2 5 8 3 3 $N = 2$
2   8   2   8   3
  4   3   5   3

New list   2 3 2 3 3 4 8 5 8
Third pass   2 3 2 3 3 4 8 5 8 $N = 1$
2 3 2 3 3 4 8 5 8
Final list   2 2 3 3 3 4 5 8 8

8 First pass   3 5 4 5 2 3 6   Swap 3 and 5
5 3 4 5 2 3 6
Second pass   5 3 4 5 2 3 6   Swap 3 and 4
5 4 3 5 2 3 6
Third pass   5 4 3 5 2 3 6   Swap 3 and 5
5 4 5 3 2 3 6   Swap 4 and 5
5 5 4 3 2 3 6   No swap
Fourth pass   5 5 4 3 2 3 6   No swap
Fifth pass   5 5 4 3 2 3 6   Swap 2 and 3
5 5 4 3 3 2 6   No swap
Sixth pass   5 5 4 3 3 2 6   Swap 2 and 6
5 5 4 3 3 6 2   Swap 3 and 6
5 5 4 3 6 3 2   Swap 3 and 6
5 5 4 6 3 3 2   Swap 4 and 6
5 5 6 4 3 3 2   Swap 5 and 6
5 6 5 4 3 3 2   Swap 5 and 6
Final list   6 5 5 4 3 3 2

Exam practice 1 (page 9)

1

R	I	W	D	P	L	A
I	D	P	L	A	R	W
D	A	I	P	L	R	W
A	D	I	L	P	R	W
A	D	I	L	P	R	W

2 a

A	B	Print
1	1	1, 1
2	8	2, 8
3	27	3, 27
4	64	4, 64
5	125	

b A always equals 1; never ending loop

3 a i

A	B	C	D	X_1	X_2	Print
1	-4	4				
			0			
				2	2	Equal roots, 2

ii

A	B	C	D	X_1	X_2	Print
2	9	9				
			9			
				$-\frac{3}{2}$	-3	Different roots, -1.5, -3

b **i** Any values where $D < 0$ or $A = 0$
   ii Line 25
     If $D < 0$ THEN
     PRINT "NO SOLS"
     GOTO M

     Line 15
     IF $A = 0$ THEN
     PRINT "NOT QUADRATIC"
     GOTO M

4

14	27	23	36	18	25	16	66
–	~	x	••	–	~	x	••

14	25	16	36	18	27	23	66
–	~	–	~	–	~	–	~

14	25	16	27	18	36	23	66

14	16	18	23	25	27	36	66

5 **a** The algorithm below is used to generate a sequence of numbers.

LINE	N	PRINT
10	6	
20		6
30	3	
40		3
50	2	
60		2
70		GOTO LINE 30
30	1	
40		1
50	0	
60		0
80		END

b

LINE	N	PRINT
10	4	
20		4
30	2	
40		2
60		2
70		GOTO LINE 30
30	1	
40		1
50	0	
60		0
80		END

6 Pivoting on the first entry gives:

<u>87</u>	64	92	35	16	41	23
<u>64</u>	35	16	41	23	[87]	[92]
<u>35</u>	16	41	23	[64]	[87]	[92]
<u>16</u>	23	[35]	[41]	[64]	[87]	[92]
[16]	[23]	[35]	[41]	[64]	[87]	[92]

7 First pass

	35			14				
		89			11			
			31			5		
				27			44	
14	11	5	27	35	89	31	44	3 swaps

Second pass

14		5		35		31	
	11		27		89		44
5	11	14	27	31	44	35	89	3 swaps

Third pass

5	11	14	27	31	44	35	89	
5	11	14	27	31	35	44	89	1 swap

8

							comp.	swaps
24	89		71	56	28	67	43	1	1
24	71	89		56	28	67	43	2	1
24	56	71	89		28	67	43	3	2
24	28	56	71	89		67	43	4	3
24	28	56	67	71	89		43	3	2
24	28	43	56	67	71	89		5	4

9

	9	4	1	6	8	7	3	comp.	swaps
After first pass	4	1	6	8	7	3	**9**	6	6
After second pass	1	4	6	7	3	**8**	**9**	5	3
After third pass	1	4	6	3	**7**	**8**	**9**	4	1
After fourth pass	1	4	3	**6**	**7**	**8**	**9**	3	1
After fifth pass	1	3	**4**	**6**	**7**	**8**	**9**	2	1
After sixth pass	**1**	**3**	**4**	**6**	**7**	**8**	**9**	1	0

SKILLS CHECK 2A (page 14)

1

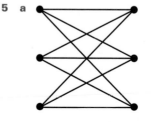

There are many other possibilities.

2 **a** **i** 5   **ii** 7   **iii** Connected
   b **i** 6   **ii** 5   **iii** Not connected
   c **i** 7   **ii** 8   **iii** Connected

3

4 **a**

b ... or ...

5 **a**

b Example

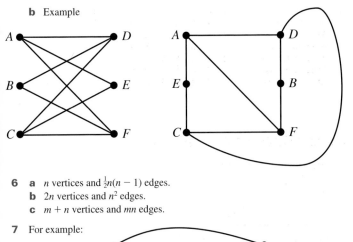

6 a n vertices and $\frac{1}{2}n(n-1)$ edges.
b $2n$ vertices and n^2 edges.
c $m + n$ vertices and mn edges.

7 For example:

If the graph is simple then there is never more than one edge directly connecting a pair of vertices. The graph K_4 has six edges, and this is the greatest number of edges that a simple graph on four vertices can have.

8 a $1 + 3 = 4$
b $6 + 0 = 6$
c $3 + 0 + 0 = 3$

SKILLS CHECK 2B (page 16)

1

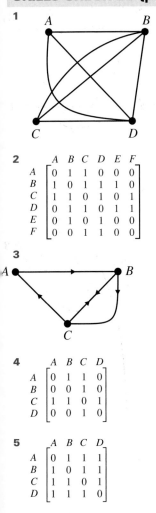

2

$$
\begin{array}{c c}
& \begin{array}{c c c c c c} A & B & C & D & E & F \end{array} \\
\begin{array}{c} A \\ B \\ C \\ D \\ E \\ F \end{array} &
\left[\begin{array}{c c c c c c}
0 & 1 & 1 & 0 & 0 & 0 \\
1 & 0 & 1 & 1 & 1 & 0 \\
1 & 1 & 0 & 1 & 0 & 1 \\
0 & 1 & 1 & 0 & 1 & 1 \\
0 & 1 & 0 & 1 & 0 & 0 \\
0 & 0 & 1 & 1 & 0 & 0
\end{array} \right]
\end{array}
$$

3

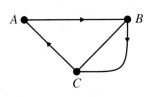

or

4

$$
\begin{array}{c c}
& \begin{array}{c c c c} A & B & C & D \end{array} \\
\begin{array}{c} A \\ B \\ C \\ D \end{array} &
\left[\begin{array}{c c c c}
0 & 1 & 1 & 0 \\
0 & 0 & 1 & 0 \\
1 & 1 & 0 & 1 \\
0 & 0 & 1 & 0
\end{array} \right]
\end{array}
$$

5

$$
\begin{array}{c c}
& \begin{array}{c c c c} A & B & C & D \end{array} \\
\begin{array}{c} A \\ B \\ C \\ D \end{array} &
\left[\begin{array}{c c c c}
0 & 1 & 1 & 1 \\
1 & 0 & 1 & 1 \\
1 & 1 & 0 & 1 \\
1 & 1 & 1 & 0
\end{array} \right]
\end{array}
$$

6

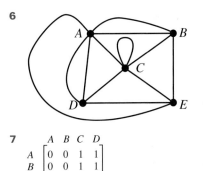

7
$$
\begin{array}{c c}
& \begin{array}{c c c c} A & B & C & D \end{array} \\
\begin{array}{c} A \\ B \\ C \\ D \end{array} &
\left[\begin{array}{c c c c}
0 & 0 & 1 & 1 \\
0 & 0 & 1 & 1 \\
1 & 1 & 0 & 0 \\
1 & 1 & 0 & 0
\end{array} \right]
\end{array}
$$

8 a There are four edges that connect to each of A, B, C and D. But there are only three edges that connect to E, so the graphs cannot be isomorphic.
b There are only three edges that connect to K, so the first graph cannot be isomorphic to the third.
If the second graph is isomorphic to the third, then $E \leftrightarrow K$ and $H \leftrightarrow L$. Reordering the second matrix gives:

$$
\begin{array}{c c}
& \begin{array}{c c c c} F & E & H & G \end{array} \\
\begin{array}{c} F \\ E \\ H \\ G \end{array} &
\left[\begin{array}{c c c c}
- & 1 & 2 & 1 \\
1 & - & 1 & 1 \\
2 & 1 & - & 2 \\
1 & 1 & 2 & -
\end{array} \right]
\end{array}
$$

So the second and third graphs are isomorphic.

SKILLS CHECK 2C (page 18)

1 a $A = 4$, $B = 3$, $C = 5$, $D = 4$, $E = 3$, $F = 4$, $G = 3$
b B, C, E and G
c $4 + 3 + 5 + 4 + 3 + 4 + 3 = 26$ 13 edges
2 a e.g. $A - B - C - A - F$
b e.g. $A - B - C - D$
c e.g. $A - B - F - G - E - D - C$
3 a There is no edge joining E to F so this is not a possible route.
b This is a path, but it is not closed (it does not join back to the start) so it is not a cycle.
c This is closed, but it passes through C twice so it is not a cycle.
4 The graph must be a tree, e.g.

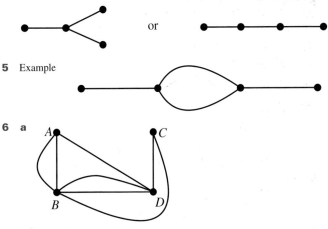

or

5 Example

6 a

b Example, $A - B - C - D$
c Example, $A - B - C - D - A$
7 a This is not possible since a graph cannot have three odd vertices.
The sum of the degrees is twice the number of edges, so the sum of the degrees cannot be odd.
b

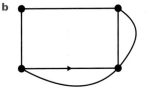

8 Example

SKILLS CHECK 2D (page 20)

1 n

2 **a** d must be an even positive integer.

 b Sum of degrees = $2 \times 12 = 24$, so d must equal 4.

3 **a** $A\,B\,E\,D\,B\,C\,D\,F\,C\,A$ (many other possibilities)

 b $A\,B\,E\,D\,F\,C\,A$ (or in reverse)

4 **a** $A-B-C-D-A$ is not an Eulerian trail because it does not use every edge in the graph.

 b $A = 4, B = 4, C = 4, D = 4$.
 These are all even, so the graph is Eulerian.

 c e.g. $A-B-D-C-A-B-C-D-A$.

5 **a** A Hamiltonian cycle only visits each vertex once (except the start and finish).

 b e.g. $A-B-C-D-A$.

6 **a** Eulerian, each vertex has degree 4 so they are all even.

 b In K_4, each vertex has degree 3. We need to remove two edges to give a graph with four vertices, each of degree 2.

7 $(3 \times 2 \times 1) \div 2 = 3$
 $(A-B-C-D-A, A-B-D-C-A$ and $A-C-B-D-A)$.

8 Six edges $\Rightarrow$ sum of degrees $= 12$. Graph is connected so each vertex has degree > 0. Graph is Eulerian so each vertex has even degree. Hence four of the vertices must have degree 2 and the fifth must have degree 4. The graph is simple, so the vertex of degree 4 connects to each of the others and these connect in pairs:

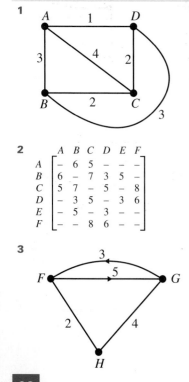

There is no Hamiltonian cycle on this graph because the vertex of degree 4 has to be passed through in connecting one part of the graph to the other part.

SKILLS CHECK 2E (page 21)

1

2

	A	B	C	D	E	F
A	–	6	5	–	–	–
B	6	–	7	3	5	–
C	5	7	–	5	–	8
D	–	3	5	–	3	6
E	–	5	–	3	–	–
F	–	–	8	6	–	–

3

4

	A	B	C	D	R	S	T	U
A	–	–	–	–	5	–	–	3
B	–	–	–	–	6	–	4	–
C	–	–	–	–	–	3	–	–
D	–	–	–	–	–	–	5	6
R	5	6	–	–	–	–	–	–
S	–	–	3	–	–	–	–	–
T	–	4	–	5	–	–	–	–
U	3	–	–	6	–	–	–	–

5 11

6 **a**

	A	B	C	D
A	–	2	2	2
B	2	–	–	1
C	2	–	–	3
D	2	1	3	–

 b $B-A-C = 4$ and $B-D-C = 4$, so the shortest distance is 4.

7 $ABCDA$ has length $x + 10 + 18 + 15 = 43 + x$
 $ABDCA$ has length $x + 13 + 18 + 12 = 43 + x$
 $ACBDA$ has length $12 + 10 + 13 + 15 = 50 \Rightarrow x = 7$.

8 **a** $8 + 2 + 14 = 24$ minutes.

 b Each Hamiltonian cycle passes through four stations (excluding the start and finish) so the journey time is 8 minutes longer than the sum of the edge weights.
 $T-P-Q-R-S-T = 20 + 8 + 7 + 10 + 18 = 63;$
 $T-P-R-Q-S-T = 20 + 12 + 7 + 6 + 18 = 63;$
 $T-P-Q-S-R-T = 20 + 8 + 6 + 10 + 15 = 59;$
 $T-P-S-Q-R-T = 20 + 14 + 6 + 7 + 15 = 62;$
 $T-P-R-S-Q-T = 20 + 12 + 10 + 6 + 14 = 62;$
 $T-P-S-R-Q-T = 20 + 14 + 10 + 7 + 14 = 65;$
 $T-Q-P-S-R-T = 14 + 8 + 14 + 10 + 15 = 61;$
 $T-Q-S-P-R-T = 14 + 6 + 14 + 12 + 15 = 61;$
 $T-Q-P-R-S-T = 14 + 8 + 12 + 10 + 18 = 62;$
 $T-Q-R-P-S-T = 14 + 7 + 12 + 14 + 18 = 65;$
 $T-R-P-Q-S-T = 15 + 12 + 8 + 6 + 18 = 59;$
 $T-R-Q-P-S-T = 15 + 7 + 8 + 14 + 18 = 62.$
 The quickest journey time is $59 + 8 = 67$ minutes.

SKILLS CHECK 2F (page 23)

1 $n - 1$

2 For example:

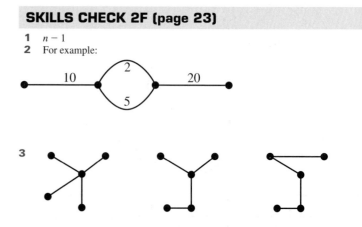

3

4 **a** A vertex of order 5 creates five 'branches', each of which must lead to at least one 'branch ending'.

 b

5 There are six vertices, so the spanning tree will have five edges and the sum of the degrees must be $2 \times 5 = 10$. But $1 + 1 + 1 + 1 + 2 + 3$ is only 9.

6 If AB is not used, the minimum spanning tree uses AC, BC and BD and has weight 35.
 If AB is used, the minimum spanning tree also uses BC and BD and has weight $23 + x$. This is at least 35, so $x \geqslant 12$.

7 **a** The ends of the branches have degree 1, so a tree can never have all its vertices of even degree.

b To travel every edge of a tree and return to the start, we must travel every edge twice. The length of the shortest closed trail is twice the weight of the spanning tree.

8 a 6 vertices
b $6 - 1 = 5$ edges
c $(1 + 1 + 1 + 2 + 3 + n) \div 2 = 5 \Rightarrow n = 2$

Exam practice 2 (page 24)

1 a 3
b i $n - 1$ **ii** $(n - 1)!$
c

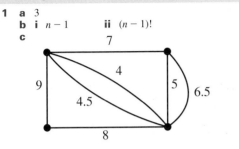

2 Graph 1: no – odd vertices (semi)
Graph 2: no – odd
Graph 3: yes – even

3 a i 4   **ii** 2   **iii** 5
b

4 a

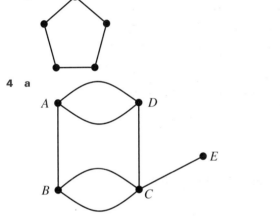

b For example,

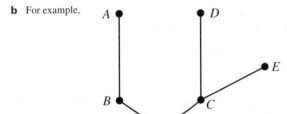

c

	A	B	C	D	E
A	0	1	0	0	0
B	1	0	1	0	0
C	0	1	0	1	1
D	0	0	1	0	0
E	0	0	1	0	0

5 a

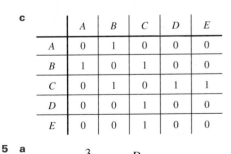

b $A - B - C - E - D - A$ (or this in reverse).
c $4 + 2 + 6 + 2 + 3 = 17$.

6 a 18
b A vertex of degree 5 is connected to each of the other vertices, so the total of the degrees cannot be less than $3 \times 3 + 3 \times 5 = 24$. We already know that it must be 18.
c

7 a There is no edge joining V to Y.
b The vertex U is passed through twice.
c This is a cycle, but it misses out the vertex W.

8 a

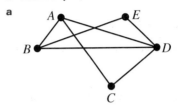

b $A - B - E - D - C - A$ or equivalent
c A spanning tree must connect all the vertices, so if AC and AD are not used then edge AB must be used. The only edge that we can use to connect C to another vertex is CD.
The edges AB and CD must be joined together and connected to vertex E using two of the edges BD, BE and DE. Any two of these will complete a spanning tree. There are three ways of choosing two of these edges (and leaving one out).
So there are three possible spanning trees that use neither of the edges AC and AD.

SKILLS CHECK 3A (page 30)

1 $BE = 6$
$AB = 8$
$EF = 8$
$BC = 9$
$FG = 9$
$FH = 9$
~~$AC = 10$~~
~~$CF = 10$~~
~~$EH = 10$~~
$CD = 11$
~~$DG = 11$~~
~~$AD = 12$~~
~~$CE = 12$~~
~~$GH = 13$~~
~~$DF = 14$~~

2 $AB = 5$
$BD = 6$
$AC = 7$
$BE = 8$
$DF = 9$
$FG = 4$
Length of tree = 39

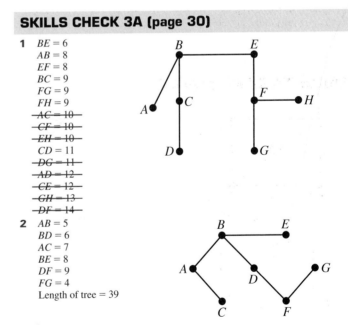

3

	A	B	C	D
A	–	12	5	10
B	12	–	(11)	18
C	(5)	11	–	11
D	(10)	18	11	–

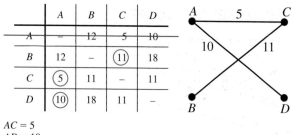

$AC = 5$
$AD = 10$
$BC = 11$ Total weight = 26

4 a Without using BE:

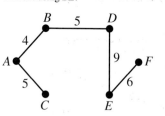

If X is greater than 9 it will not be included, but the least value is $X = 9$ since then there are two minimum spanning trees, one of which is the tree shown above.

b If BE must be included then X is less than 9.

5 a When Kruskal's algorithm is applied the least weight edge is chosen first and the next least weight will then be chosen since two edges cannot form a cycle in a simple graph.

b Example   or

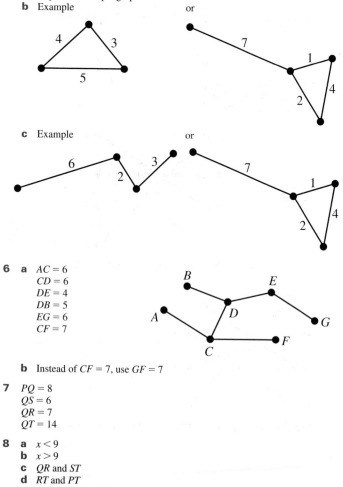

c Example   or

6 a $AC = 6$
$CD = 6$
$DE = 4$
$DB = 5$
$EG = 6$
$CF = 7$

b Instead of $CF = 7$, use $GF = 7$

7 $PQ = 8$
$QS = 6$
$QR = 7$
$QT = 14$

8 a $x < 9$
b $x > 9$
c QR and ST
d RT and PT
e $19 < $ weight $\leqslant 28$

Exam practice 3 (page 32)

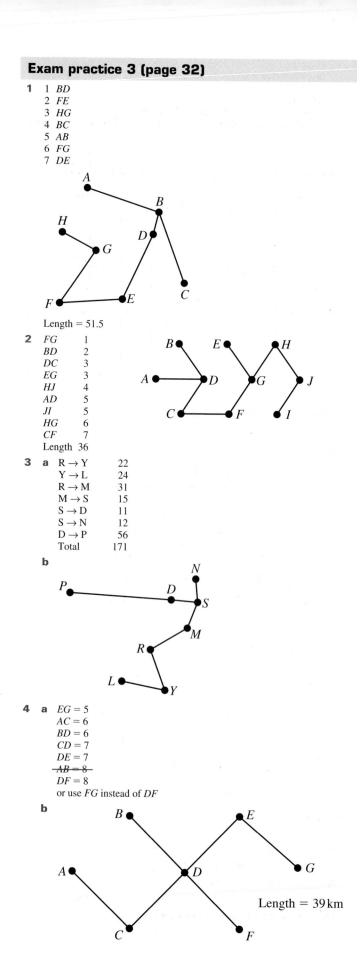

1 1 BD
2 FE
3 HG
4 BC
5 AB
6 FG
7 DE

Length = 51.5

2 FG 1
BD 2
DC 3
EG 3
HJ 4
AD 5
JI 5
HG 6
CF 7
Length 36

3 a $R \rightarrow Y$ 22
$Y \rightarrow L$ 24
$R \rightarrow M$ 31
$M \rightarrow S$ 15
$S \rightarrow D$ 11
$S \rightarrow N$ 12
$D \rightarrow P$ 56
Total   171

b

4 a $EG = 5$
$AC = 6$
$BD = 6$
$CD = 7$
$DE = 7$
$AB = 8$
$DF = 8$
or use FG instead of DF

b

Length = 39 km

5 a $PQ = 6$
$QS = 7$
$QR = 8$
$ST = 10$
$TU = 9$ Length of tree = 40 metres
b The new edge will replace $ST = 10$, giving a tree of length $= 30 + x$ metres.
So $x = 5$.

6

	A	B	C	D	E	F	G	H
A	–	~~6~~	–	~~4~~	–	~~8~~	–	~~5~~
B	~~6~~	–	~~3~~	~~6~~	⑤	–	~~7~~	~~7~~
C	–	③	–	–	~~6~~	–	~~6~~	–
D	④	~~6~~	–	–	–	~~7~~	–	–
E	–	~~5~~	~~6~~	–	–	–	⑤	–
F	~~8~~	–	–	~~7~~	–	–	–	④
G	–	~~7~~	~~6~~	–	~~5~~	–	–	②
H	⑤	~~7~~	–	–	–	~~4~~	~~2~~	–

$AD = 4$ Vertices added in the order A, D, H, G, F, E, B, C
$AH = 5$
$HG = 2$
$HF = 4$ Total weight = 28
$GE = 5$
$EB = 5$
$BC = 3$

7 a

	A	B	C	D	E	F
A	–	~~3~~	~~4~~	~~5~~	~~6~~	~~7~~
B	③	–	~~2~~	~~4~~	~~8~~	~~9~~
C	~~4~~	②	–	~~5~~	~~7~~	~~8~~
D	~~5~~	④	~~5~~	–	~~9~~	~~7~~
E	⑥	~~8~~	~~7~~	~~9~~	–	~~6~~
F	~~7~~	~~9~~	~~8~~	~~7~~	⑥	–

$AB = 3$
$BC = 2$
$BD = 4$
$AE = 6$
$EF = 6$

b

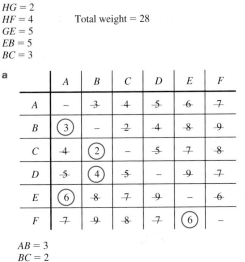

8 $VW = 5$
$VX = 6$
$XZ = 5$ or $WY = 5$
$YZ = 4$

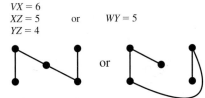

There are two possible minimum spanning trees.

1

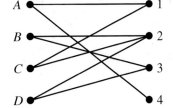

2

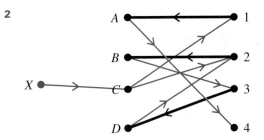

Minimum alternating path is $X - C - 1 - A - 4$.

3

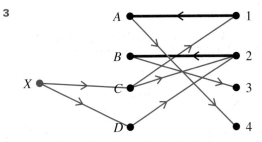

One minimum alternating path is $X - C - 1 - A - 4$
(other possibilities exist).
Matching is: $A - 4, B - 2, C - 1$.

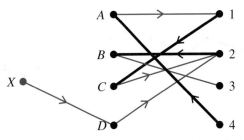

From this position a minimum alternating path is $X - D - 2 - B - 3$.

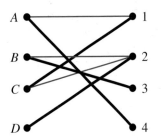

This gives the complete matching: $A - 4, B - 3, C - 1, D - 2$.

4 a

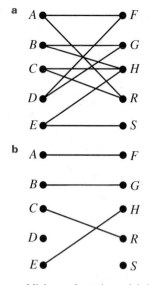

b

Minimum alternating path is $D - G - B - H - E - S$.
Complete matching: $A - F, B - H, C - R, D - G, E - S$.

c Only two of the children have their first choice.

5 a

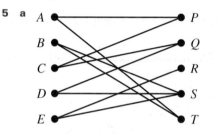

b The easiest way to find the alternating path is to start at R and work backwards until either A or C is reached.

Either $R - E - S - B - T - A$ or $R - E - S - D - Q - C$

These give either   Adam = Tuna   or   Adam = Pie
                Briony = Salad   Briony = Tuna
                Charlie = Pie   Charlie = Quiche
                Debbie = Quiche   Debbie = Salad
                Ed = Ravioli   Ed = Ravioli

6 $T - 1 - R - 5$ and $W - 4 - U - 2$ to give $R = 5, S = 3, T = 1, U = 2, W = 4$

7

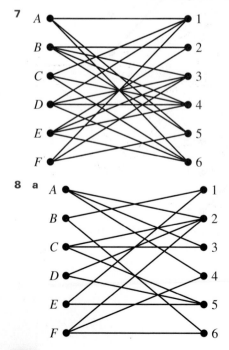

8 a

b Example, alternating $D - 2 - F - 6$ to give $A = 4, B = 1, C = 5, D = 2, F = 6$.

c Example, alternating path $E - 5 - C - 3$ to give the complete matching $A = 4, B = 1, C = 3, D = 2, E = 5, F = 6$.

d Any of $A = 2, B = 6, C = 3, D = 5, E = 1, F = 4$
   or $A = 3, B = 6, C = 2, D = 5, E = 1, F = 4$
   or $A = 3, B = 6, C = 5, D = 2, E = 1, F = 4$
   or $A = 4, B = 6, C = 3, D = 5, E = 1, F = 2$

Exam practice 4 (page 40)

1 a

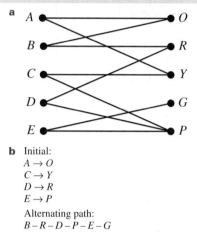

b Initial:
$A \to O$
$C \to Y$
$D \to R$
$E \to P$

Alternating path:
$B - R - D - P - E - G$
(breakthrough)
or $B \to O, A \to Y, C \to P$
     $E \to G, (D \to R)$

Complete match:
$A \to O$		or	$A \to Y$
$B \to R$			$B \to O$
$C \to Y$			$C \to P$
$D \to P$			$D \to R$
$E \to G$			$E \to G$

2 a i

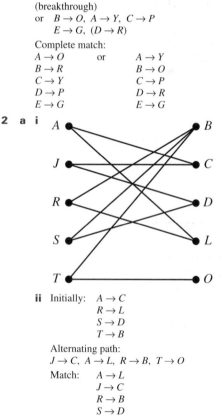

ii Initially: $A \to C$
              $R \to L$
              $S \to D$
              $T \to B$

Alternating path:
$J \to C, A \to L, R \to B, T \to O$
Match: $A \to L$
        $J \to C$
        $R \to B$
        $S \to D$
        $T \to O$

3 a

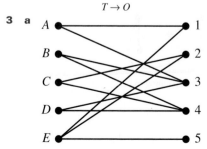

b $(A-3, B-4, E-1)$

$C-2, D-3, A-1, E-5$

Match:

$A-1, B-4, C-2, D-3, E-5$

4 a

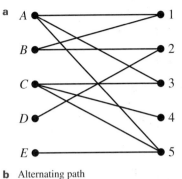

b Alternating path

$D-2-B-1-A-3-C-4$

$A = 3$

$B = 1$

$C = 4$

$D = 2$

$E = 5$

5 a

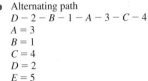

b Alternating path

$D-F-A-P$

Alan = Parallel bars

Boris = Horse

Carl = Rings

Derek = Floor mat

c Alan = Parallel bars

Boris = Rings

Carl = Floor mat

Derek = Horse

6 a

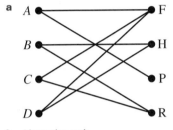

b Alternating path

$W-C-S-D$

$R = B$

$S = D$

$T = E$

$W = C$

c $R = C$

$S = D$

$T = B$

$W = E$

d The first matching

1 a

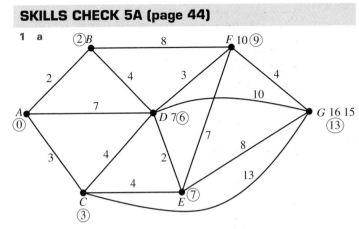

Minimum journey time = 13 hours

Route: $A-B-D-F-G$

b For example, would need to stop for breaks.

It would take time travelling through the towns.

May get delayed or held up in traffic jams.

2 FG cannot be used so must reach G from E.

Minimum time = $7 + 8 = 15$ hours.

3 Journey time = 14 hours, this is achieved by reaching F in 10 hours and then

$10 + 4 = 14$.

Route: $A-B-F-G$ or $A-D-F-G$ or $A-C-D-F-G$

Since these are all available but $A-B-D-F-G$ is not available, it must be

road BD that is closed.

4

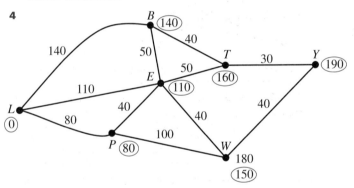

5 a

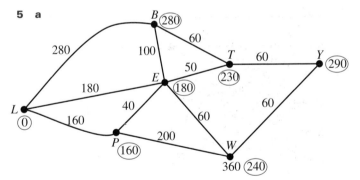

b Working shown on network.

Quickest route takes 290 minutes: $L-E-T-Y$.

6 a

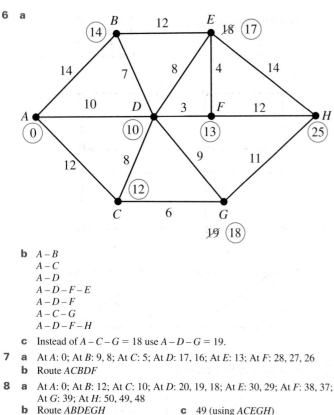

b $A - B$
  $A - C$
  $A - D$
  $A - D - F - E$
  $A - D - F$
  $A - C - G$
  $A - D - F - H$

c Instead of $A - C - G = 18$ use $A - D - G = 19$.

7 a At A: 0; At B: 9, 8; At C: 5; At D: 17, 16; At E: 13; At F: 28, 27, 26
b Route $ACBDF$

8 a At A: 0; At B: 12; At C: 10; At D: 20, 19, 18; At E: 30, 29; At F: 38, 37;
  At G: 39; At H: 50, 49, 48
b Route $ABDEGH$ **c** 49 (using $ACEGH$)

9 a At A: 0; At B: 12; At C: 10; At D: 22; At E: 15; At F: 30, 29, 28;
  At G: 20, 19; At H: 50, 45, 39, 38
b Route $ABDFH$ **c** 36 (using $DFHG$)

10 a At A: 0; At B: 9, 8; At C: 5; At D: 17, 16; At E: 18, 17; At F: 24, 22;
  At G: 26, 25; At H: 30, 29
b Route $ACBDEFGH$ **c** $x < 17$

Exam practice 5 (page 46)

1 a

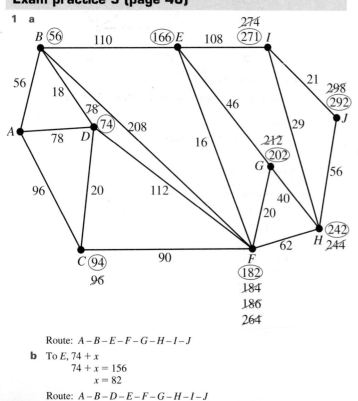

  Route: $A - B - E - F - G - H - I - J$

b To E, $74 + x$
    $74 + x = 156$
        $x = 82$

  Route: $A - B - D - E - F - G - H - I - J$

2 a

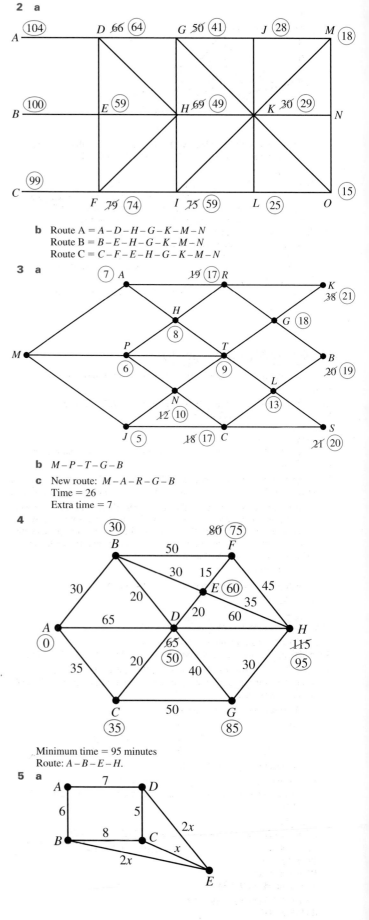

b Route A $= A - D - H - G - K - M - N$
  Route B $= B - E - H - G - K - M - N$
  Route C $= C - F - E - H - G - K - M - N$

3 a

b $M - P - T - G - B$

c New route: $M - A - R - G - B$
  Time $= 26$
  Extra time $= 7$

4

  Minimum time $= 95$ minutes
  Route: $A - B - E - H$.

5 a

b

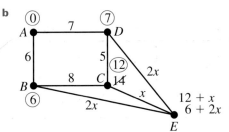

Shortest route is either of length $12 + x$ miles or of length $6 + 2x$ miles.

c Route must pass through $C \Rightarrow 12 + x < 6 + 2x \Rightarrow x > 6$.

6 a $7 - x + 8 > 12 \Rightarrow x < 3$
$2x - 1 + 9 > 12 \Rightarrow 2x > 4 \Rightarrow x > 2$ So $2 < x < 3$

b F is the second vertex to become permanent since it gets the temporary label $7 - x$ and this must be less than the temporary label 7 at B.
Since $2 < x < 3$, the permanent label at F is between 4 and 5.

c Since the permanent label at F is between 4 and 5, we then assign a temporary label of value between 8 and 9 at E.
The value 7 at B then becomes permanent, but this has no effect on any of the other labels. The smallest temporary label at C is now 9, at E is $11 - x$ and at D is still 12.
But $2 < x < 3$ so $8 < 11 - x < 9$, and E becomes permanent next, followed by C.

SKILLS CHECK 6A (page 50)

1 Vertices A and B are odd, to be traversable the network must have all even vertices.

2 Must repeat the shortest path joining A to B. This is $AB = 2$ hours.
Sum of weights on network $= 79$.
So minimum journey time $= 79 + 2 = 81$ hours.
A suitable route would be:
$A - B - F - G - C - A - B - D - F - E - G - D - E - C - D - A$ (many other possibilities).

3 This requires either an Eulerian or a semi-Eulerian graph, so either 0 or 2 odd vertices. A and B are odd, so minimum $= 79$ hours and journey would end at B.

4 The first can be paired with any of the other seven, this leaves six vertices to pair off. The first of these six can be paired with any of the remaining five; this leaves four vertices to pair off. The first of these four can be paired with any of the other three; this leaves two vertices which then form the final pair.
$\Rightarrow 7 \times 5 \times 3 \times 1 = 105$ possible pairs

5 A, D, E and F are odd.

$AD = 300$	$AE = 400$	$AF = 450$
$EF = \underline{\ 50}$	$DF = \underline{150}$	$DE = \underline{100}$
350	550	550

Minimum is achieved by repeating AD and EF.

Sum of lengths of all corridors $= 2000$ metres.
So minimum distance the teacher must walk is $2000 + 350 = 2350$ metres.

6 a A, B, C, F, G and H are all odd vertices. Because the route must start at A and end at H these vertices must be odd, so we need to pair B, C, F and G to make them even.

The least weight connecting paths are:

$BC = 15$	$BF = 10$	$BG = 16$
$FG = \underline{12}$	$CG = \underline{\ 6}$	$CF = \underline{11}$
27	16	27

Sum of weights in network $= 130$

So least weight route has weight $130 + 16 = 146$

b Route must start at A, use every edge once, repeat edges BD, DF, CG and end at H.
Example:
$A - B - E - H - G - C - A - D - B - D - E - F - D - C - G - D - F - H$

7 a $BC + FE = 21$ **b** $ABFBCECDEFA$
$BE + CF = 37$
$BF + CE = 20$
Minimum $68 + 20 = 88$

8 a Repeat CF; Total $68 + 19 = 87$
b $BAFBCECDEFE$

9 a Odd vertices   **b** $AB + CD = 20$
$AC + BD = 18$
$AD + BC = 19$
Minimum $57 + 18 = 75$

10 a 2
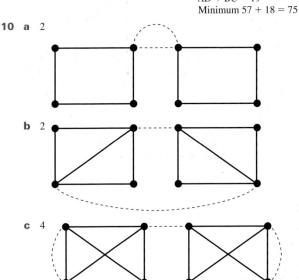

b 2

c 4

Exam practice 6 (page 52)

1 a
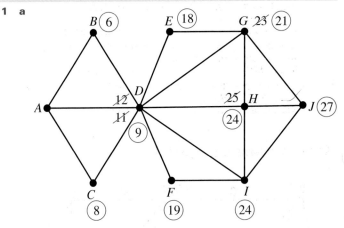

Route: $A - C - D - E - G - J$

b Min $=$ all lengths $+$ repeat $A \rightarrow J = 133 + $ (their 27) $= 160$

2 a i $IJ = 31$
ii $EF = 63$
iii $AC = \sqrt{(100^2 + 100^2)} \ (= 141)$
$AE = 31$

b Odd vertices I, J, K, L
Min $31 + 31 = 62$
Total $=$ each path $+ 62$

$=\ \ 31 \times 4 = 124$
$63 \times 4 = 252$
$31 \times 4 = 124$
$100 \times 2 = 200$
$20 \times 4 = \underline{\ \ 80}$
780
$+ \underline{\ 62}$
842

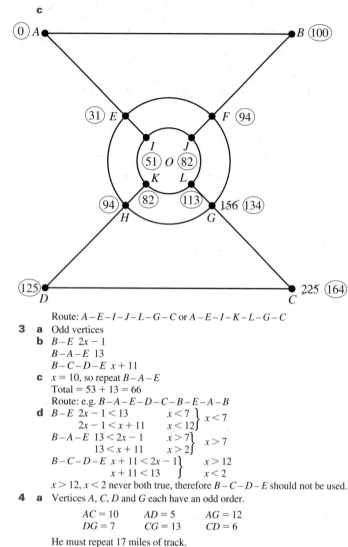

Route: $A - E - I - J - L - G - C$ or $A - E - I - K - L - G - C$

3 a Odd vertices
  b $B - E$ $2x - 1$
    $B - A - E$ 13
    $B - C - D - E$ $x + 11$
  c $x = 10$, so repeat $B - A - E$
    Total $= 53 + 13 = 66$
    Route: e.g. $B - A - E - D - C - B - E - A - B$
  d $B - E$ $2x - 1 < 13$ $x < 7$ $\Big\}$ $x < 7$
        $2x - 1 < x + 11$ $x < 12$
      $B - A - E$ $13 < 2x - 1$ $x > 7$ $\Big\}$ $x > 7$
        $13 < x + 11$ $x > 2$
      $B - C - D - E$ $x + 11 < 2x - 1$ $\Big\}$ $x > 12$
        $x + 11 < 13$ $x < 2$
    $x > 12$, $x < 2$ never both true, therefore $B - C - D - E$ should not be used.

4 a Vertices A, C, D and G each have an odd order.

$AC = 10$	$AD = 5$	$AG = 12$
$DG = 7$	$CG = 13$	$CD = 6$

  He must repeat 17 miles of track.
  b The tracks AC, DE and EG are travelled twice.

5 a

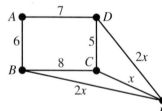

  b Vertices B, C, D and E each have an odd order.
    In the case when $x = 3$:

$BC = 8$	$BD = 12$	$BE = 6$
$DE = 6$	$CE = 3$	$CD = 5$

  Repeat BE and CD to give a route of length 11 more than the sum of the arc weights $= 11 + 41 = 52$ miles.
  c In the case when $x > 8$:

$BC = 8$	$BD = 13$	$BE = 8 + x$
$DE = 5 + x$	$CE = x$	$CD = 5$

  Route is of length $41 + 13 + x = 54 + x$ miles.

6 a C and F are odd vertices, so the shortest route will use every edge once and repeat the shortest path joining C to F.
  b Sum of weights $= 58 + x$.
    Shortest path joining C to F is either CAF or CDF.
    CAF has eight $16 - x$ with weight $7 + 2x$.
    This gives a total weight of either 74 or $65 + 3x$.
    Since the lengths of the footpaths are positive, $2x - 1 > 0 \Rightarrow x > 0.5$.
    Hence the minimum possible weight is greater than 66.5, giving a distance of 6650 metres.

SKILLS CHECK 7A (page 56)

1 $7 + 4 + 8 + 7 + 8 + 13 + 3 = 50$ hours.
  Solution to TSP: $\leqslant 50$ hours.

2 a $A - B - D$ is only $4 + 3 = 7$ km
  b $C - A - D$ (via B) $= 3 + 7 = 10$ km but $C - B - D$ is only $2 + 3 = 5$ km

  $$\begin{array}{c|cccc}
   & A & B & C & D \\
  \hline
  A & - & 4 & 3 & 7 \\
  B & 4 & - & 2 & 3 \\
  C & 3 & 2 & - & 5 \\
  D & 7 & 3 & 5 & - \\
  \end{array}$$

  c $A - B - C - D - A = 4 + 2 + 5 + 7 = 18$ km
  d $A - B - C - B - D - B - A$

SKILLS CHECK 7B (page 58)

1 $A - B - D - F - G - E - C - A$
  $2 + 4 + 3 + 4 + 8 + 4 + 3 = 28$ hours.
  Solution to TSP: $\leqslant 28$ hours.

2 a $A - C - B - D - A = 15$
  b $B - C - A - D - B = 15$
    $C - B - D - A - C = 15$
    $D - B - C - A - D = 15$
    The tours are all the same, in this example the starting point makes no difference.

3 Route starts $A - C - B - D$ but then route gets stuck and cannot return directly to A. Method fails to find a tour because their was no edge joining A to D. The network was not complete.

4 a 3
  b $ACBDA - 37$
  c $CB + BD + (AB + AC) = 9 + 11 + 15 = 35$

SKILLS CHECK 7C (page 61)

1 Minimum spanning tree = 20 hours

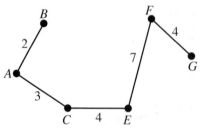

  Two least-weight edges from D are $3 + 4 = 7$
  Lower bound $= 20 + 7 = 27$ hours

2 $27 \leqslant$ TSP $\leqslant 28$. The quickest journey time for a tour through all the vertices is 28 hours. The route found using the nearest neighbour method in Skills Check 7B question **1** is suitable.

3 a $A - B - D - F - E - C - A = 150$ metres
  b Minimum spanning tree = 93 metres
    $BD = 20$, $BF = 23$, $BE = 24$, $BC = 26$
    Two shortest edges from A are $14 + 18 = 32$ metres.
    Lower bound $= 93 + 32 = 125$ metres

4 a The nearest neighbour method gives tours of length 15, so this is an upper bound.
  b The minimum connector for B, C and D is $BC = 2$, $BD = 3$ and the two shortest edges to join A back in are $AB = 4$ and $AC = 3$, giving a lower bound of $5 + 7 = 12$.
  c The length of the shortest cycle through all the vertices is between 12 and 15 (inclusive).

5 a $ABCBDA = 57$ **b** 57
    $BACDB = 58$
    $CABDC = 58$
    $DACBD = 57$

6 a Delete $A = 55$, Delete $B = 54$ **b** 56
    Delete $C = 54$, Delete $D = 56$

7 a $56 \leqslant$ Optimal tour $\leqslant 57$
  b Optimal tour
  c There is a mistake.

Exam practice 7 (page 62)

1 a Minimum spanning tree [Mn = Milnrow, Md = Middleton]:

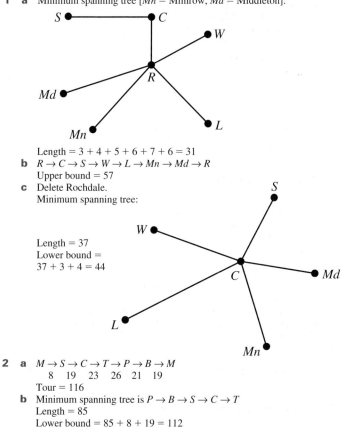

Length = $3 + 4 + 5 + 6 + 7 + 6 = 31$

b $R \to C \to S \to W \to L \to Mn \to Md \to R$

Upper bound = 57

c Delete Rochdale.

Minimum spanning tree:

Length = 37

Lower bound =

$37 + 3 + 4 = 44$

2 a $M \to S \to C \to T \to P \to B \to M$

 $\quad\;\; 8 \quad 19 \quad 23 \quad 26 \quad 21 \quad 19$

Tour = 116

b Minimum spanning tree is $P \to B \to S \to C \to T$

Length = 85

Lower bound = $85 + 8 + 19 = 112$

c $112 \le D \le 116$

3 a i $44 + 56 + 66 + 64 + 60 + 48 = 338$

 ii Tour; can be improved

b Off $\to 1 \to 3 \to 5 \to 4 \to 2 \to$ Off

 $\quad\quad 44 \quad 50 \quad 62 \quad 60 \quad 62 \quad 52$

Total = 330

c Minimum spanning tree:

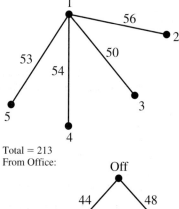

Total = 213

From Office:

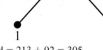

Off

Lower bound = $213 + 92 = 305$

4 a $8 + 10 + 9 + 9 + 3 = 39$ minutes.

b $A - E - C - D - B - A = 3 + 6 + 9 + 15 + 8 = 41$ minutes.

c The lower value is the better upper bound, so an upper bound for Alan's minimum journey time is 39 minutes. MST $\le$ 39.

d Minimum spanning tree for vertices A, B, C, D uses edges AB, AC and AD and has total weight 19 minutes.

Two least weight edges from E are EA and EC with a total weight of $3 + 6 = 9$ minutes.

So lower bound = $19 + 9 = 28$ minutes.

5 a $A - B - D - E - G - F - C - A = 4 + 4 + 4 + 3 + 7 + 6 + 10 = 38$ miles.

b The nearest neighbour algorithm assumes that the network is on a complete graph. If the graph is not complete then sometimes the nearest neighbour algorithm gets 'stuck' and cannot visit all the vertices without repeating some of them.

c Minimum spanning tree for vertices A, B, C, E, F and G uses edges AB, BE, EG, GF and FC and has total length 25 miles.

Two least weight edges from D are DB and DE with a total weight of 8 miles. So lower bound = $25 + 8 = 33$ miles.

d For example, $A - B - E - G - F - C - D - A$, which has length 36 miles.

6 a $A - C - D - B - E - F - A$

$2 + 3 + 5 + 6 + 8 + 18 = 4200$ metres

b Minimum spanning tree for $\{A, B, C, D, E\}$ uses edges AC, AB, CD, BE and has total length 1400 metres.

Two shortest edges from F are DF and EF with a total length of 1700 metres.

Lower bound = 3100 metres

SKILLS CHECK 8A (page 67)

1 a $b = c$

 $a < b$

b $b = 0$

 $a > 2c$

c $a \le 0.25(a + b + c) \Rightarrow 0.75a \le 0.25b + 0.25c \Rightarrow 3a \le b + c$

2 a x = number of Xmas cards Auntie makes

 y = number of Yachts cards Auntie makes

b $2x + y \le 10$

c $20x + 30y \le 180 \Rightarrow 2x + 3y \le 18$

d $x \ge 0$ and $y \ge 0$

e $25x + 25y$ (or scale to get $x + y$, for example)

3 a Each 'snow scene' card takes Holly $3\frac{3}{4}$ minutes and each 'trees' card takes her $6\frac{2}{3}$ minutes. She has $7 \times 60 = 420$ minutes available each week.

So, $3\frac{3}{4}s + 6\frac{2}{3}t \le 420 \Rightarrow 45s + 80t \le 5040 \Rightarrow 9s + 16t \le 1008$

b $6s + 4t \le 180 \Rightarrow 3s + 2t \le 90$

c Maximise $P = 110s + 105t$ (in pence)

or scale to get $22s + 21t$, for example.

SKILLS CHECK 8B (page 70)

1 a $(0, 0) \to x + 2y = 0$

 $(80, 0) \to x + 2y = 80$

 $(30, 50) \to x + 2y = 130$

 $(20, 50) \to x + 2y = 120$

 $(0, 30) \to x + 2y = 60$

The maximum value is 130.

b $x \ge 0$

 $y \ge 0$

 $y \le 50$

 $x + y \le 80$

 $y - x \le 30$

2 a

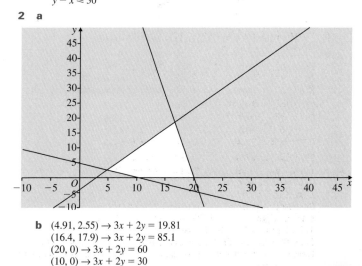

b $(4.91, 2.55) \to 3x + 2y = 19.81$

 $(16.4, 17.9) \to 3x + 2y = 85.1$

 $(20, 0) \to 3x + 2y = 60$

 $(10, 0) \to 3x + 2y = 30$

3 a

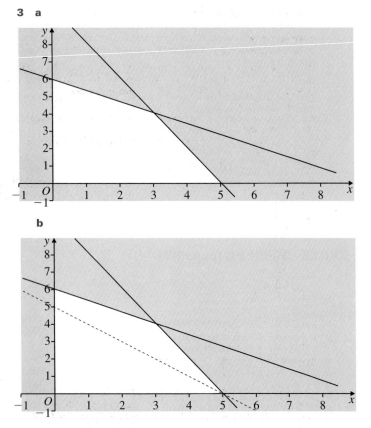

b

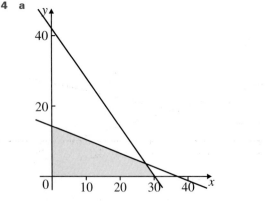

c By sliding the objective line, the maximum profit is achieved at the vertex (3, 4).

Auntie should make 3 Xmas cards and 4 Yachts cards. This uses all her time and all her card. It will give her a profit of £1.75.

4 a

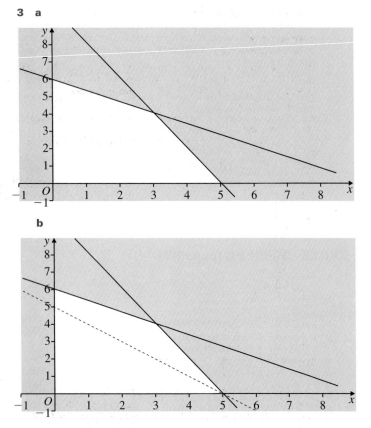

Line cross axes at (30, 0), (0, 45) and (37.33), 0), (0, 15.75)

b $x = 27.13$ and $y = 4.30$ (to 2 d.p.) giving $P = 3408.67$.

c

x	y	$27x + 64y$	$3x + 2y$	P	
27	4	985	89	3363	
28	4	1012	92	not feasible	
27	5	1049	91	not feasible	
28	3	948	90	3367	*
29	1	847	89	3266	
30	0	810	90	3270	
25	5	995	85	3250	
23	6	1005	81	3137	

The maximum value of P is 3367 at $x = 28$ and $y = 3$.

5 a

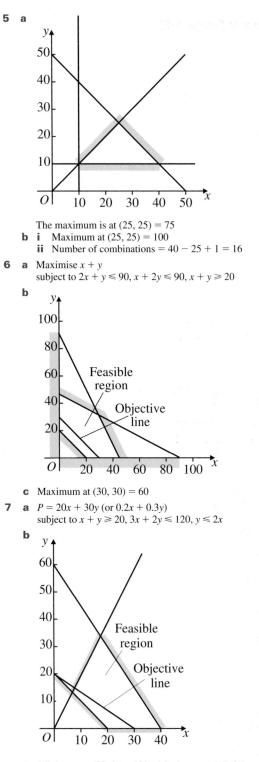

The maximum is at (25, 25) = 75

b i Maximum at (25, 25) = 100

ii Number of combinations = $40 - 25 + 1 = 16$

6 a Maximise $x + y$
subject to $2x + y \leqslant 90$, $x + 2y \leqslant 90$, $x + y \geqslant 20$

b

c Maximum at (30, 30) = 60

7 a $P = 20x + 30y$ (or $0.2x + 0.3y$)
subject to $x + y \geqslant 20$, $3x + 2y \leqslant 120$, $y \leqslant 2x$

b

c Minimum at (20, 0) = 400p, Maximum at (17, 34) = 1540p

8 Maximise $3x + 5y + 10z$
subject to $30x + 40y + 50z \leqslant 1440$
$4x + 4y + 5z \leqslant 120$
$x \geqslant \dfrac{66}{100}(x + y + z) \Rightarrow 2x \geqslant 3(y + z)$
$y \geqslant z$
$x + y + z \geqslant 15$

1 $x + 2y + 3z \geqslant 30$
$2x + 3y + 5z \geqslant 50$
$3x + 3y + 4z \geqslant 40$
$6x + 8y + 12z \leqslant 200$
$2x + 3y + 5z \geqslant \frac{2}{5}(6x + 8y + 12z)$
$\Rightarrow z \geqslant 2x + y$

2 a $2x + 4y \leqslant 50$
$3x + y \leqslant 24$
$x + y \leqslant 20$
$x \geqslant 2, y \geqslant 2$
$(T =) 20x + 25y$

b

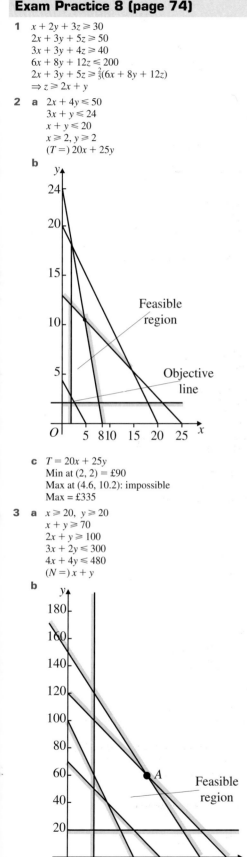

Feasible region

Objective line

c $T = 20x + 25y$
Min at $(2, 2) = £90$
Max at $(4.6, 10.2)$: impossible
Max $= £335$

3 a $x \geqslant 20, \ y \geqslant 20$
$x + y \geqslant 70$
$2x + y \geqslant 100$
$3x + 2y \leqslant 300$
$4x + 4y \leqslant 480$
$(N =) x + y$

b

Feasible region

c i   Max no. is $x = 20, \ y = 100$
Total $= 120$
ii   Point A is $(60, 60)$
No. of solutions is $(20, 100) \rightarrow (60, 60) = 41$

4 a   Each cream cake costs 60p, four doughnuts cost £1 so they are 25p each, and the éclairs work out as 40p each. The expression $60c + 25d + 40e$ is the total cost in pence, which is what Tara wants to minimise.

b   The total number of cakes must be at least 10, so $c + d + e \geqslant 10$.

c   If $d = 8$ then Tara needs to minimise $60c + 40e$ subject to $c + e \geqslant 2$, with c and e both integers and e a multiple of 3.
Two cream cakes costs £1.20 and three éclairs also cost £1.20, so either will cost Tara £1.20 + £2 = £3.20.

d   Twelve doughnuts would only cost £3.

5 a

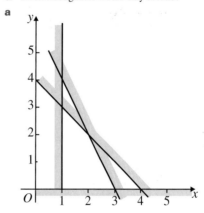

b   Vertices of feasible region are $(1, 0)$, $(3, 0)$, $(2, 2)$ and $(1, 3)$.
Either by sliding a line of the form $x + 2y =$ constant or by checking the vertices we find the maximum value of $x + 2y$ to be 7 when $x = 1$ and $y = 3$.

6 a $4x + 15y$ **b** $4x + 15y \leqslant 90$ **c** $x \geqslant 5y$

d

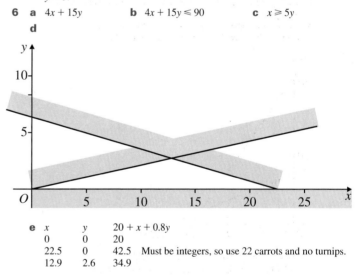

e

x	y	$20 + x + 0.8y$	
0	0	20	
22.5	0	42.5	Must be integers, so use 22 carrots and no turnips.
12.9	2.6	34.9	

1 a

<u>24</u>	<u>16</u>	38	49	10	15	52	28
<u>16</u>	<u>24</u>	<u>38</u>	49	10	15	52	28
<u>16</u>	<u>24</u>	<u>38</u>	<u>49</u>	10	15	52	28
<u>16</u>	<u>24</u>	38	<u>49</u>	<u>10</u>	15	52	28
<u>10</u>	<u>16</u>	24	38	<u>49</u>	15	52	28
<u>10</u>	<u>15</u>	16	24	38	<u>49</u>	52	28
<u>10</u>	<u>15</u>	16	24	38	<u>49</u>	<u>52</u>	<u>28</u>
10	15	16	24	28	38	49	52

b   1 comparison, 1 swap

c   7 comparisons, 4 swaps

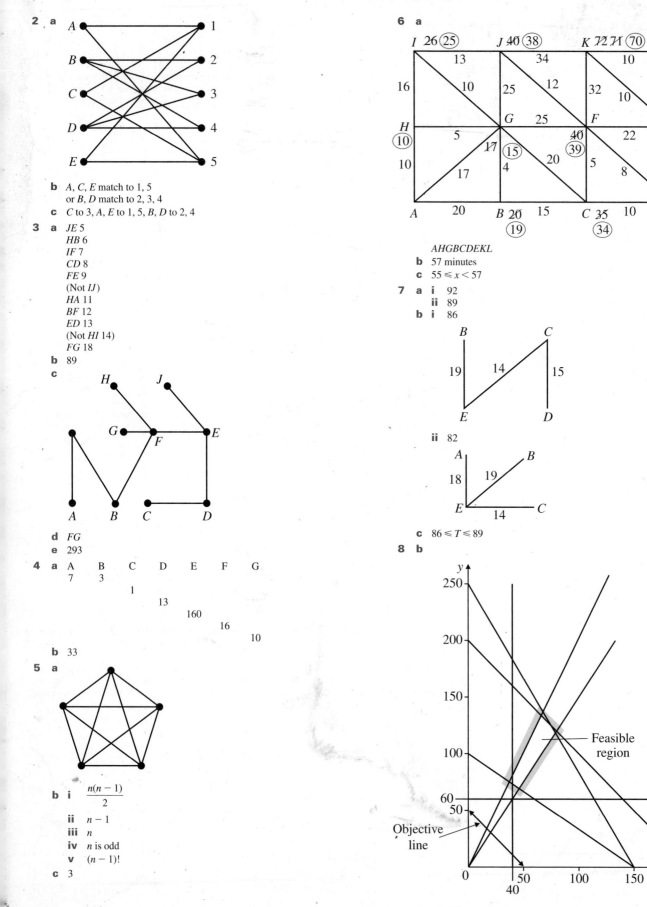

2 a

b A, C, E match to 1, 5
or B, D match to 2, 3, 4

c C to 3, A, E to 1, 5, B, D to 2, 4

3 a JE 5
HB 6
IF 7
CD 8
FE 9
(Not IJ)
HA 11
BF 12
ED 13
(Not HI 14)
FG 18

b 89

c

d FG

e 293

4 a

A	B	C	D	E	F	G
7	3					
		1				
			13			
				160		
					16	
						10

b 33

5 a

b i $\dfrac{n(n-1)}{2}$

ii $n-1$

iii n

iv n is odd

v $(n-1)!$

c 3

6 a

AHGBCDEKL

b 57 minutes

c $55 \leqslant x < 57$

7 a i 92
ii 89
b i 86

ii 82

c $86 \leqslant T \leqslant 89$

8 b

Feasible region

Objective line

c $y \geqslant 60$

d £93.30, $x = 67$, $y = 133$